Gordon King
2602 Capistrano St.
Blacksburg, VA 24060

The Oldie
ANNUAL 2015

OLDIE PUBLICATIONS

'Just occasionally your medication may have a mild hallucinogenic effect...'

Published by Oldie Publications Ltd
65 Newman Street, London W1T 3EG
www.theoldie.co.uk

Copyright © 2014 Oldie Publications Ltd

ISBN: 978-1-901170-22-1

A catalogue record for this book is available from the British Library

Printed and bound in China by C&C Offset Printing

Acknowledgements
The Oldie would like to thank all the writers, illustrators
and cartoonists whose work is reproduced in these pages

Editorial production team: Sonali Chapman, Joe Buckley and John Bowling

ANNUAL 2015

WITH AN INTRODUCTION BY
RICHARD INGRAMS

WORLD'S WORST DUMPS

CONTENTS

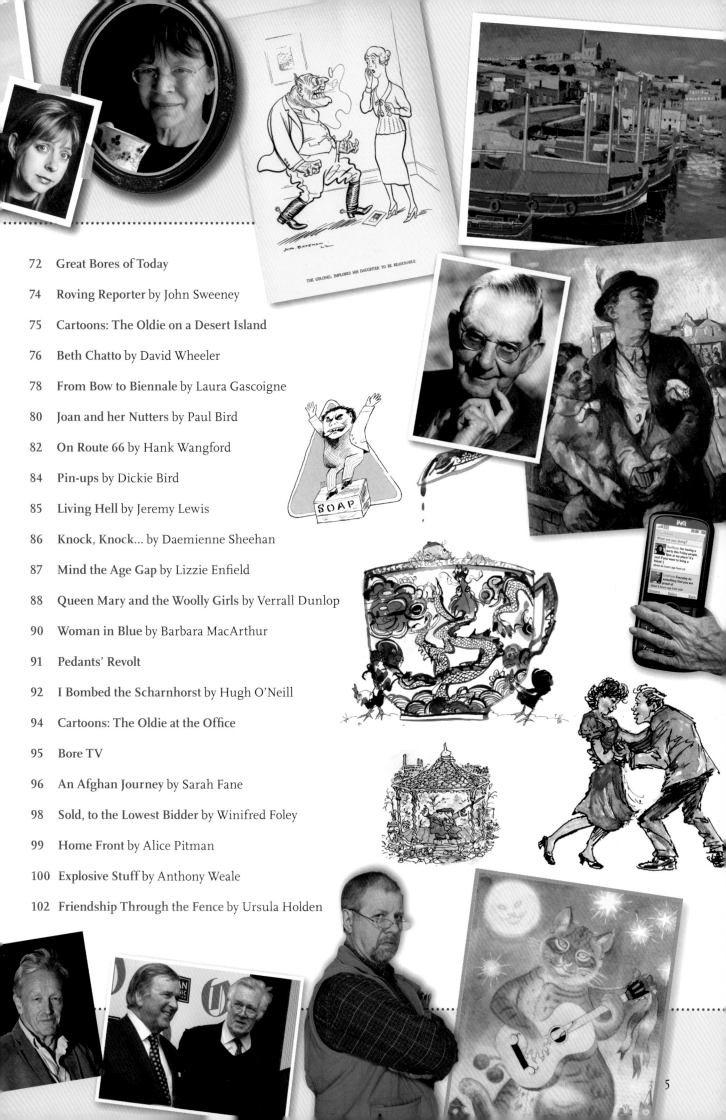

'We've been asked to investigate a report that a large dog is causing trouble in the district'

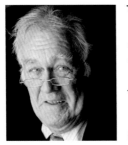

Welcome to The Oldie Annual for 2015
I know that many of you regular readers will be familiar with the kind of book you can expect but I would nevertheless crave your attention for a moment, as not all these annuals are necessarily identical in layout and appearance, let alone content.

We hope you will enjoy the reading experience we are offering. You will find a rich variety of articles and illustrations – some old, some new – all reflecting *The Oldie*'s tradition of printing not only the work of well-known names but those whom other magazines might dismiss as mere amateurs.

Now sit back, relax and enjoy your read.

Richard Ingrams

Olden life

What was... ITMA?

BACK ROW, LEFT TO RIGHT: Francis Worsley (producer), Charles Shadwell (music), Fred Yule, Dino Galvani, Horace Percival, Ted Kavanagh (scriptwriter)
MIDDLE ROW, LEFT TO RIGHT: Clarence Wright, Dorothy Summers, Tommy Handley, Jack Train, Sidney Keith
FRONT ROW, LEFT TO RIGHT: Paula Green (probably) and Diana Morrison

GOOD QUESTION: catchphrases from it are used sometimes but very few people now under the age of 70 can have listened to it. *ITMA* was a radio programme (*It's That Man Again* – a reference to Hitler's pre-war territorial demands) which ran for 300 episodes between 1939 and 1949. During that period the passion for important-sounding acronyms was born; thus, mockingly, ITMA. The star of the show was Tommy Handley, whose speed and clarity of diction made, for some reason, everything he said sound funny, although – a genial and modest man – he left it to others to get the big laughs. In the shows he was always an official of some kind, Mayor of Foaming-at-the-Mouth, Minister in the Office of Twerps, etc, cheerfully unabashed by his inability to do anything at all, because of constant interruption by a succession of (unexplained) visitors. There was Ali Oop trying to sell him naughty postcards – 'I go – I come back'; Funf, the ever-present and useless German spy; two workmen paralysed by their English politeness – 'After you, Claude.' 'No, after *you*, Cecil'; and Colonel Chinstrap, perpetually in search of a drink. 'Colonel, you have been treated most shabbily.' 'A glass of Chablis, sir? I don't mind if I do.'

Almost every public institution was mocked. To me, an adolescent and snobbish critic, there was something hysterical in the laughter of the studio audience, but even I detected some mysterious gratitude in it, and blessed relief. Also, 'mocked' is not the right word – 'made light of' would be better, and this is what listeners seemed to love. Their number swelled to 13 million. The programme was light, and it was a dark time: no TV of course, theatres shut, food rationed, bombings;

no recourse but the radio, listened to from behind black-out curtains. Some thought it nonsense, and 'nonsense' it was, language used for the sound of it more than for its meaning. An example: the office cleaner, Mrs Mopp – 'Can I do you now, sir?' pronounced with heavy innuendo to which Handley was immune ('She's never been the same since Gladstone made her Miss 1888') – always bade him farewell with the letters T.T.F.N. ('Ta ta for now') to which on one occasion Handley replies, 'N.W.A.W.W.A.S.B.E.' 'What's that, sir?' 'Never wash a window with a soft-boiled egg.' If that doesn't make you smile, or even laugh, *ITMA* is not for you. Bessie Braddock MP complained in Parliament that the programme was nothing but 'a welter of bad puns'. It was, and my father Ted, who wrote the scripts, was delighted.

In 1974 the Woburn Press published *The ITMA Years*, which along with their history contains four scripts chosen from the ten years of

BENEFITS

K.J.Lamb

'Your tiny handout is frozen'

programmes. To read these is to be astonished at the sheer speed. No sequence lasts for more than a few seconds, there is no time to notice the silliness. Signor So-So, the comic Italian – 'Oh Mr Handlebar, I am delightful to see you' – announces the arrival of some Scotsmen 'wearing squirts'. 'You mean skirts, women don't wear squirts, they marry them.' And so on, and on, but always so fast there was no time to ponder.

In 1949 Tommy Handley died suddenly of a brain haemorrhage, and *ITMA* died with him. I saw, fifty years later, TTFN written on the inside of a steamed-up coach window, a farewell to a friend outside. One of Handley's many harridans, forever berating him for inefficiency and shiftlessness, was always interrupted by her yapping dog, to which she cries, 'Down, Upsie!', and exits. I heard a man say those words to his over-excited dog in a pub a couple of years ago. He must have been about fifty, so he couldn't know *why* he said it. How long does a catchphrase last, its source long gone? What is sure is that nothing important changes, certainly not our desperate need for genial nonsense.

So great was the national affection *ITMA* aroused that six thousand people attended Tommy Handley's memorial service in St Paul's, two thousand on the steps outside hearing it broadcast. Press photographs printed in *The ITMA Years* reminded me of this. I had forgotten the extent of this love, and I shouldn't have.

P J KAVANAGH

Modern life

What is ... hot-desking?

NATURALLY, I consider myself one of life's free-range chickens. The open range is the place for me, not cooped up in poorly lit and cramped accommodation, seething with fear and resentment. That's how I view the office, with its battery chickens chained to desks, pecking away at ephemera and memoranda. But even that fate is contingent on the poor broilers getting a desk at all in this age of 'hot-desking'.

If only hot-desking had been around in Goldilocks's time. Instead of running for her life, she could simply have admonished her hirsute persecutors: 'Baby Bear, that is not your bed; it is everyone's bed. And the same goes for your porridge and the place at the table. Besides, what on earth are you bears doing living in a house in the first place? You should be off down the woods doing what you do best – eating wildlife film cameramen and defecating.'

Of course, for us miserable hot-deskers, finding a place in the office that's 'just right' is rarely an option.

It's 'first come, first served' when it comes to getting a desk these days, and the bosses always make sure there are more people than desks. This is mainly thanks to one of the many iniquitous aspects of hot-desking. For the management, it is a litmus test of reliability and punctuality. The goody-two-shoes nab all the best desks close to the boss's office because they get in at the crack of dawn, while the lazybones all have to squat on the unkempt desks close to the disabled toilets or wander about all day looking for a place – refugees in their own office. They are the 'undesked'.

Once upon a time, I had my own desk. I can't say it was much to look at. Somewhere under the clutter was a dusty computer, a pile of scarcely credible expenses claims and a photograph of the Family Deplume in straw hats on the Costa del Sol. But at least it was *my* desk – until some management swine snatched it away and I was forced to work in a 'hot-desking environment'.

Like most bad ideas, hot-desking was dreamt up by that unholy alliance of architects and consultants. As we know, this is a very bad mix indeed and responsible for all manner of terrible things from Welwyn Garden City to Legoland. Insecurity is the ethos behind hot-desking. As Alfie might have said at the end of the film of the same name, 'I don't have a desk. And if you don't have that, you've got nothing. So what's it all about?'

According to the consultants, a desk equals work security and therefore, naturally, the other three riders of the bosses' apocalypse: complacency,

incompetence and sloth. Desks discourage 'churn'; in other words, they do not encourage insecurity or instil in the breast of employees a deep desire to leave and seek a job that comes with its own desk. Desks have a detrimental effect on the impact of fear, and fear, like greed, is good.

This explains why people in the office are terrified of leaving their desks for long in case others take their place. This has led to all sorts of disgusting habits such as eating 'al desko'. In my office most people eat 'al desko', slurping overpriced runner bean and hoisin quail soup from the staff canteen or nervously gulping down a baked potato with some brown fluffy substance – possibly tuna, possibly coronation chicken, possibly something emitted by either a tuna or a chicken – deposited on top.

The goody-two-shoes nab all the best desks while the lazybones have to squat on the unkempt ones by the disabled toilets...

No one ever takes responsibility for any desk. Why should they when someone else will occupy it tomorrow? Consequently, like hotel rooms, they are always left in a filthy mess with broken computers going unreported and other people's important files and correspondence ending up in the bin. Hot-desking creates confusion and discontinuity that is harmful to individual and organisation alike. Even for architects.

I heard of one story where three hot-desking architects moved around their office so much that their separate plans for a bordello especially for men restricted in the underpants department, an asylum for delusional psychopaths and a hostel for distressed bearded folk became hopelessly muddled together. Of course the three clients were livid although the resulting scheme did prove ideal as a new headquarters for the Liberal Democrats.

Many of us pray there will be some New Age of Common Sense and that we victims of the office diaspora will eventually be restored to our own desks. But as we say down at the range – don't hold your clucking breath.

NORMAN DEPLUME

'Obesity has its advantages'

Pearls of Wisdom

COLIN THUBRON

The eminent travel writer and novelist talks to **MELANIE McFADYEAN**

COLIN THUBRON CBE is one of our greatest writers, with many awards and twenty-one books to his name, most of them travel writing but also seven novels. 'My travel books spring from curiosity about worlds which my generation has found threatening: China, Russia, Islam – perhaps from a desire to humanise and understand them,' he has written. 'The novels seem to be reactions against this, and mostly arise from more introverted, personal concerns, often being set in enclosed places.' After Eton he went into publishing and, briefly, TV. For *To a Mountain in Tibet* (Chatto, 2011), he climbed to 18,600 feet, following the pilgrims' trail around Mount Kailas in the Himalayas. Aged 75, he is married and lives in London.

Your curiosity seems undimmed by age
I suppose it's a kind of optimism – the feeling that there will always be something interesting and fascinating round the corner. I don't go into a country with a sense of understanding, however heavy my research has been. So the books, I hope, transmit expectations from an author who is taking the reader through a journey of discovery – including its innocence, mistakes, misapprehensions and understandings. So perhaps that is why the vitality appears to remain.

Do the journeys get easier?
I may know a bit more about how to travel wisely, but I don't feel any more in command of my subject when I start out. I don't feel fear before a journey, just excitement and curiosity and an odd sense of invulnerability – but of course there are always anxieties before leaving about what's going to happen, and especially about whom you are going to meet. My books are predicated on people. A journey is dead unless you experience the culture – and that is mostly experienced through the people I meet.

I am appalled looking back to my earliest books, on Damascus for example, because I couldn't speak Arabic. I now have the basis of Russian and Mandarin, and awful tourist Arabic. Mandarin and Russian take you through a great deal of Asia – most of central Asia has a lingua franca of Russian. There is great delight in an interesting conversation with someone who lives in the land in which you are travelling. People's lives are always extraordinary.

What do you take with you?
As little as possible. Before leaving, I lay out everything I think I need, then ask myself do I *really* need that? The answer is almost always no. But I always take a compass: my sense of direction is very strong – but usually wrong.

Do you feel wiser with age?
I suppose I feel I'm an old fool really.

I feel less and less certain about anything. There's a quote I love from Newton, towards the end of his life: 'I do not know what I may appear to the world, but to myself I seem to have been only like a boy playing on the seashore, and diverting myself in now and then finding a smoother pebble or a prettier shell than ordinary, whilst the great ocean of truth lay all undiscovered before me.'

What is troubling about ageing?
You have less time, and time becomes more precious. The proportion between what's possible and what you apprehend to be out there somewhere is more and more weighted against your ever discovering anything much, so it becomes more important to travel, to discover, to read, because while there's less time, the burden of what has to be understood is greater. You feel you could have led numberless other lives.

In *Among the Russians* you say you have 'a restless inner life and a distrust of belonging'. Why the distrust of belonging?
Probably I meant distrust of belonging to anywhere specific, to anyone specific. That would have grounded me, and at that age I wouldn't have wanted to be grounded. Belonging meant a narrowing down of possibility.

Was it some early experience that made you feel that way?
Did you think the death of my sister made me distrust loving? I don't think so. But in my teens I was quite Christian. I wished to hold onto that, and even after my sister's death – I was only 19 when she died – I wanted to believe in an afterlife.

Coincidentally I started my first job as an apprentice in a publishing firm the week she died, and there were all these books. I became ravenously fascinated by everything and alert and alive in ways I hadn't been before. My teenage Christianity seemed too constrictive. I had built it up as a delicate edifice and then one day the whole thing crashed to bits. It was a tremendous relief, really, because in a sense I'd been excusing Christianity, its concepts of the afterlife and hell and so on.

When you wrote *To a Mountain in Tibet*, your mother had died, leaving you the last of your family. Did you find an accommodation with death?
My journey's motive was more visceral

than intellectual but I realise that I was testing the idea of what we think of as an individual. In Hindu Buddhism there is no personal survival, no soul, no God. What survives is the weight of good or evil in the world, that gets carried on as karma, which has no individual property. It put one's own life in perspective – one's self isn't so important. On this sort of journey you're walking the earth, it's a pilgrimage in a sense. It could have made a lovely narrative if it had ended in enlightenment or catharsis, but it didn't. In some way it reconciled me to the idea of my own death. Yet I don't close the gates to anything, because I think life is entirely incomprehensible and mysterious. I really don't understand a thing. There's that old story of the Viking feast. A bird flies in from the dark across the hall and goes out the other end through an open door into darkness again. That's a synonym for human existence – a creature comes in out of total darkness and disappears into darkness. Why we happen to be here now seems infinitely curious.

Do you get lonely on those journeys?
Loneliness is incomprehensible to me. I love solitude. But I got married for the first time in 2011 and now I would probably feel lonely without my wife.

Do you regret having had no children?
Not achingly. You fantasise about an ideal daughter but when I look at other people's children I'm not greatly encouraged. I don't know how good a father I'd have been. Solitude is essential to the sort of work I do.

Are you fit enough in your seventies to go on with these arduous journeys? Don't you feel more afraid?

'Nobody understands why I'm such a bastard...'

Nobody is as well as they wish to be at my age. But one's mental state is far more important than one's physical state. You can go on doing stuff if you wish it and you're curious enough. I'm naturally fairly fit. I like tennis but I don't play as much as I should. I've got a bad knee but have had that since I was seven. It hurts a bit on the tennis court and going downhill.

Have you had any accidents?
I had a car crash in 1978. I'd like to say it was in Uzbekistan, but it was in East Grinstead. I had a broken back and shoulder. I was lucky not to be paralysed. I was on my back for weeks, but immobility has always been rather good for me because my mind goes wandering and concocts things. I concocted the idea that I wanted to walk along the Great Wall of China.

Have you got another big journey planned?
The next journey? I don't know. I don't like having to decide on one. I like it to insist on itself out of nowhere. I'm writing a novel at the moment. It's big and complicated, which may be a product of age, as it's much more contemplative than my previous ones.

There's melancholy running through your books as well as comedy.
Most people notice the melancholy, not the humour.

You don't seem like a melancholic fellow...
I'm not melancholic day to day. There's too much to be fascinated by, to enjoy – but there is an underlying melancholy, which is logical. As the Buddhist says, from all that he loves, man must part.

At what age are we old?
Old age is whatever's older than you by five years. I've been shocked into realising my age a few times. On the tube occasionally I am offered a seat, usually by a young woman. I think there must be someone behind me with grey hair, or hair even whiter than mine. My instinct is to say 'no thank you', but it would be more gracious to accept. The idea of a freedom pass is grotesque, but I've accepted the grotesque because it makes life easier and I'm grateful for it.

How would you complete the phrase 'life is...'?
...idiotically short.

OFF THE RAILS

Commuting is a perilous business, writes **JAMES MICHIE**

It began the moment I got my Senior Citizen's railcard – a series of haunting experiences on public transport which have left me a prematurely hunched and nervous traveller.

On the first occasion I was gazing out of the train near Didcot, recalling that this was the very stretch of landscape I had been passing 15 years before when I had hungoverly swallowed a large dollop of marmalade full of slivers of glass; how I had had to wrestle with the decision whether to get out at Reading and present myself at a hospital, or to chance it and keep my appointment in London; how the waiter had gravely offered to deduct the marmalade from the breakfast bill (oh, dear, dead days)… when *phunk!* and some other slivers of glass fell from the window between my feet and those of two newspaper-reading men opposite me. There was a pause and the papers were lowered. 'I say, that was a bullet, wasn't it?' remarked one. 'Definitely a bullet,' agreed the other.

There was a long, phlegmatically British pause. 'Ought we to report it to somebody or other?' 'Can't actually see a bullet,' said Basil Radford (by now we were all self-consciously playing parts in *The Lady Vanishes*). 'They'll only hang about for ages in Reading. Let's not make a fuss.' 'Good point,' conceded Naunton Wayne, and again the papers were raised. A second crucial decision about broken glass had been taken in my railway life.

Immediately afterwards I experienced a disturbing week on the Metropolitan tube line. On Monday, in a packed carriage, I was holding my small son in my arms, caressing him clumsily on his fretful way to school, when a Scotch voice rang out: 'Look at the way he's playing with the wee laddie! It's a disgrrrace!' All heads turned, while I tried to juggle Edward into a more 'normal' position. 'There he goes – he's at it again!' cried the terrible Old Person from Fife. I owed my escape from lynching to some large, motherly women who took my side.

The next day I was button-holed by a man in khaki shorts who, as if I were his ally, asked me at the top of his voice if I didn't agree that the carriage was filthy and that there were far too many black faces in it. I got out at the next station – the first time I had ever alighted at Royal Oak.

Friday was the climax. I was sitting minding my own business (never mind what it was) when I noticed that the middle-aged man next to me

'And these ones are stupid'

was gently leaning sideways to say something. He was conventionally dressed, his eyes were unglazed, there were no traces of foam around his lips, no suspicion of drink or drugs in the air. 'Do you see those people over there?' he asked, pointing to three unexceptional tourists in mackintoshes standing ten feet away. I said I did. 'Well, I could easily kill them all with my hands.' The nature of his message was so unexpected that I felt like the curate who has just seen his bishop park chewing-gum on the altar-rail. 'Oh?' I vouchsafed. This clearly didn't satisfy him. 'You know, it doesn't take very long to kill somebody with your hands. I could do that lot in about four minutes.' I fled – Royal Oak again, damn it – searching for a parting shot, but the words that emerged from my mouth were grotesquely inane: 'The best of British luck, sir,' I said.

After that, I took to travelling self-protectively, as if I were dozing. The result, of course, was that I actually went to sleep – on the Bakerloo line, just before Queen's Park, where the train terminated. When I woke up, I was alone in a stationary carriage, in a vast, silent, crepuscular shed, a sort of train dormitory. I could end here, with myself talking to myself and night deepening, but what in fact happened was that after half an hour I was discovered and released by a man who seemed more frightened of me than I was of him.

From now on, I shall never travel without sandwiches, book, torch, whistle, miniature radio, blanket and 'Deaf and Dumb' lapel badge. Watch out for me.

TOP CHUMPS

Simply cut out the Chumps below and glue them to a suitable hard backing. Buy *The Oldie* regularly and you'll be amazed how soon you have a complete set of Top Chumps – ready to do battle with your top CHUMS!!

Get collecting now to make sure of a complete set!!

ESTHER RANTZEN

CHUMPFILE
★ Unfortunate teeth — 99%
★ 2010 election flop — 100%
★ Ghastly Wilcox husband — 90%
★ Obscene parsnips — 98%
★ Child abuse obsession — 93%
★ 'Strictly' tango fiasco — 95%

FATHER CHRISTMAS

CHUMPFILE
★ Repetitive catchphrase — 100%
★ Scruffy beard — 90%
★ Chimney fetish — 92%
★ Cruelty to reindeers — 94%
★ Roof damage — 93%
★ Foot in mouth — 99%

GWYNETH PALTROW

CHUMPFILE
★ Children Apple and Moses — 100%
★ Bum-revealing dress — 92%
★ Crap films — 95%
★ Silly avocado recipe — 96%
★ Oscars blubbing — 100%
★ 'Conscious uncoupling' — 99%

JUSTIN WELBY

CHUMPFILE
★ Speaking in tongues — 100%
★ Comic hat — 95%
★ Tribal dance inauguration — 98%
★ Oil executive — 95%
★ Old Etonian — 100%
★ Buddhist Prince George — 95%

MARY PORTAS

CHUMPFILE
★ Ginger barnet — 100%
★ 'Queen of Shops' — 84%
★ Sapphic leanings — 96%
★ Westfield link — 99%
★ Cameron babe — 97%
★ Jargon peddler — 100%

MICHAEL GOVE

CHUMPFILE
★ Crap education reforms — 99%
★ NUJ striker — 95%
★ Iraq War hawk — 99%
★ Fishlike face — 92%
★ House-flipper — 100%
★ Blabbering wife — 98%

SIMON COWELL

CHUMPFILE
★ Pectoral implants — 85%
★ Vote-rigging charge — 95%
★ Black toilet paper — 99%
★ Gratuitous rudeness — 98%
★ Colonic irrigation — 93%
★ Won't change nappies — 100%

Old Filth

This short story by **JANE GARDAM** *was the original inspiration for her popular trilogy of Old Filth novels about the life of the inimitable Sir Edward Feathers*

Illustrated by Robert Geary

Old Filth had been a delightful man. The occasional kink, but a delightful man. A self-mocking man. The name had been his own invention. A joke against himself, now an old joke but he had been the one to think of it. 'Failed In London Try Hong Kong.' Good old legal joke.

He was Old Filth, QC, useful and dependable advocate, who would never have made judge in England. Never have made judge anywhere, come to that, for it was not what he had ever wanted. 'Failed' was his joke, for he had had exactly the career he had planned, to practise at the English bar but live as close to China as possible.

He'd been born in Shanghai more than eighty years ago, into a diplomatic family, brought up by adoring, bony Chinese ayahs in their long slinky black dresses, tight buns of black hair scraped back into the nape of the neck. They had filled him with love and superstitions and tangled forests of fiery folk tales he had loved. Old Filth spoke Mandarin and when he did you heard an unsuspected voice. All his life he had kept a regard for Chinese values, the courtesy, the hospitality, the respect for money, the decorum, the importance of food, the discretion, the cleverness. He married a Scotswoman born in Peking. She was dumpy and tweedy with broad shoulders but she too spoke some Mandarin and liked Chinese ways. She had a Chinese passion for jewellery. Her strong, Scottish fingers rattled the trays of jade in the market, stirring the stones about like pebbles on a beach. 'When you do that,' Old Filth would say, 'your eyes are almond-shaped.' Poor old Betty, he often thought now. She had died after their retirement to Dorset.

And why ever Dorset? Nobody knew. Some tradition perhaps. But if any pair of human beings had been born to be expats, members of the Cricket Club, the Jockey Club, stalwarts of the English lending library, props of St James's church, they were Filth and Betty. People you'd say who'd always be able to keep some servants, ever be happy hosts to any friend of a friend who was visiting the Colony. When you thought of Betty you saw her at her round rosewood table looking about her to see if plates were empty, tinkling her little bell to summon the smiling girls in their household livery of identical cheongsam dresses. Such perfectly international people, Old Filth and Betty. Ornaments to every memorial service in the Anglican cathedral that in the last years were falling on them thick and fast.

Was it the thought of having to survive in Hong Kong on a pension then? But the part of Dorset they had chosen was very far from cheap, and surely Old Filth must have stashed away a packet? Another of the reasons, he had always said so jollily, for not becoming a judge. And they had no children. No responsibilities. No one to come home for.

Or was it – the most likely thing – 1997? Was it the unbearable-ness of being left behind to bow to the barbarians? The unknown Chinese who would now be feeding them sweets and telling them fairy tales? Neither of them was keen on the unknown. Already, some years before they left, English was not being spoken in shops and hotels so often or so well. Many faces disappeared to London and Seattle and Toronto and rich people's children had vanished to English boarding schools. Big houses on the Peak were in darkness behind steel grilles. At Betty's favourite jeweller the little girls threading beads who still looked sixteen though she had known them twenty years, looked up more slowly now when she walked in. They still kept their fixed smiles, but found fewer good stones for her. Chinese women she knew had not the same difficulty.

So, suddenly, Old Filth and Betty were gone, gone forever from the sky-high curtain-drops of glittering lights, gold and soft green and rose, from the busy waters of the harbour and the perpetual drama of every sort of boat, junks and oil-

'It's just the pre-op bonding routine'

tankers and private yachts and the ancient and comforting dark green Star ferries that chugged back and forth to Kowloon all day and most of the night. 'This deck accommodates 319 passengers.' Filth had loved the certainty of the '19'.

So they were gone, moved far from any friend, to a house deep in the Donheads on the Wiltshire/Dorset border, an old low stone house that could not ███████████ s gate. A rough drive climbed up to it and ██████████ e house sat on a small plateau looking down over ████████ every sort of coloured English tree. Far away the horizon was a long scalpel line of milky chalk down dappled with shadows drawn across it by the clouds above. No place in the world could be less like Hong Kong.

Yet it was not so remote that a doctor might start suggesting in a few years time that it would be kind to the social services if they were to move nearer civilisation. There was a village half a mile up the hilly road that passed their gate, and half a mile in the other direction, also up a hill, for their drive ran down into a dip, was a church and a shop. There were other, if invisible, more modern houses in the trees. There was even a house next door, its gate alongside theirs, its drive curving upwards in the same way and disappearing in the same way out of sight. So they were secluded but not cut off.

And it worked. They made it work. Well, they were people who would see to it that the end of their lives worked. They changed. They discarded much. They went about very little. But they put their hearts into becoming content, safe behind the lock on their old farm-house door that could never be left accidentally on the latch. Old Filth gardened and read thrillers and biographies and worked now and then in his tool shed. He kept his QC's wig in its black and gold oval box on the hearth like a grey cat in a basket, but as nobody but Betty was there to be amused he moved it after a time to his wardrobe to lie with his black silk stockings and buckled shoes. Betty spent time sewing and looking out of the window at the trees. They went to the supermarket most weeks in their modest car and a woman came in four times a week to clean and cook and do the laundry. Betty said the legacy Hong Kong had left them was the inability to do their own washing.

After Betty died Old Filth took everything from her jewel box and sold it. He was leaving all his money to the Barristers' Benevolent Association, he said, because nobody felt much benevolence towards barristers. It was sad really that there was no one to appreciate the little joke. Nice man. Always had been.

It was the cleaning lady who destroyed it all. One morning, letting herself in with her door-key, talking even before she was over the threshold. 'Well,' she said, 'what about this then? You never hear anything in this place. Next door must have moved and there's removal vans and new stuff being moved in all up and down the drive. They say it's another lawyer from Singapore, like you.'

'Hong Kong,' said Old Filth, automatically and as usual.

'Hong Kong then. They'll be wanting help but they're out of luck. I'm well-suited here, you're not to worry. I'll find them someone. I've enough to do.'

A few days later Old Filth enquired if she'd heard anything more and was told, courtesy of the village shop, the new neighbour's name. It was indeed the name of another Hong Kong lawyer and it was the name of the only man in either his professional or private life that Old Filth had ever detested. The extraordinary effect this man had had upon him over thirty years ago and for many years after – and it had been very much noticed and the usually cautious Filth had not cared – was like the venom sprayed out from the mouths of the dragons in his old nannies' stories.

And the same had gone for Terry Veneering's view on Old Filth. And nobody knew why. It was almost a chemical, physical thing. Old Filth, kind Old Filth and swashbuckling Veneering did not 'have words', they spat poisons. They did ▪▪ cross swords, they set about them with scimitars. Old Filth believed that jumped-up Terry Veneering was all that was wrong with the English masters of the Colony – arrogant, blustering, loud, cynical, narrow and far too athletic. Without such as him, who knows? He treated the Chinese as if they were invisible, flung himself into pompous rites, strutted at ceremonials, cringed before the Governor, drank too much.

He was Old Filth, QC, useful and dependable advocate, who would never have made judge

In court he was known for treating his opponent to spates of personal abuse. Once, in an interminable case against Old Filth, about a housing estate on the New Territories that had been built over a Chinese graveyard and that mysteriously refused to prosper, he spent days sneering at primitive beliefs. Or so Old Filth said. What Veneering said about Old Filth he never enquired but there was mutual, cold, seething dislike.

Somehow or other Veneering got away with everything. He bestrode the Colony like a Colossus, booming on at parties about his excellence. On a state visit by the Queen he was rumoured to have told her all about his boy at Eton. Later it was 'my boy at Cambridge', then 'my lad in the Guards'. Betty loathed him and Old Filth's first thought when he heard that Veneering had become his new neighbour was, 'Thank God Betty's gone.' His second thought was, 'I shall have to move.'

However, the next door house was as invisible as Old Filth's, even its garden secret behind a long stand of firs that grew broader and taller all the time. Even when leaves of other trees fell there was no sight or sound of him.

'He's a widower living alone,' said the cleaning lady. 'His wife was a Chinese.' Old Filth remembered then that

Continues over page ☞

Veneering had married a Chinese woman. Strange to have forgotten. Why did the idea stir up such hatred again? He remembered the wife now, her downcast eyes and the curious chandelier earrings she wore. He remembered her at a race-course in a bright yellow silk dress, Veneering alongside, great coarse golden fellow, six foot two, with his strangled voice trying to sound public school.

Old Filth dozed off then with this picture before him, wondering at the clarity of an image thirty years old when what happened yesterday receded into utter darkness. He was eighty-three now. Veneering must be almost eighty. Well, they could keep their own corner. They need never meet.

Nor did they. The year proceeded along, and the next one. A friend from Hong Kong called on Old Filth and said, 'I believe Terry Veneering lives somewhere down here, too. Do you ever come across him?'

'He's next door. No. Never.'

'Next door? My dear fellow –'

'I'd like to have moved away.'

'But you mean you've never –'

'No.'

'And he's made no – gesture?'

'Christopher, your memory is short.'

'Well, I knew you were... You were both irrational in that direction, but –'

Old Filth walked his friend to the gate. Beside it stood Veneering's gate, overhung with ragged yews. A short length of drain-pipe was attached to Veneering's gate to take the morning newspaper, identical to the one that had been attached to Old Filth's gate for many years. 'He copied my drain-pipe,' said Old Filth. 'He never had an original notion.'

'I have half a mind to call.'

'Well, you needn't come and see me again if you do,' said courteous Old Filth.

In his car the friend considered the mystery of the fixations that survive dotage and how wise he had been to stay in Hong Kong. 'You don't feel like a visit?' he asked out of the window. 'Why not come back for Christmas? It's not so much changed that there'll ever be anywhere like it.'

But Old Filth said that he didn't stir at Christmas. Just a taxi to the White Hart at Salisbury for luncheon. Good place. Not too many paper hats and streamers. 'Hong Kong is still all streamers,' said the friend. 'I remember Betty with streamers tangled up in her gold chains.' But Old Filth just thanked him and waved him off.

And thought of him again on Christmas morning, waiting for the taxi to the White Hart, watching from a window whose panes were almost blocked with snow, snow that had been falling when he'd opened his bedroom curtains five hours ago at seven o'clock. Big, fast, determined flakes. They fell and fell. They danced. They mesmerised. After a few minutes you couldn't tell if they were going up or down. Thinking of the road at the end of the drive, the deep hollow there, he wondered if the taxi would make it. At 12.15 he thought he might ring and ask, but waited until 12.30 as it seemed tetchy to fuss. He found that the telephone was not working.

'Ah,' he said. 'Ha.'

There were mince-pies and a ham-shank. A good bottle somewhere. He'd be all right. A pity though. A break with tradition. He stood staring at the Christmas cards. Fewer again this year. As for presents, nothing except his cousin at Hainault.

Always two handkerchieves. Well, more than he ever sent her. He must remember to send some flowers or something.

He picked up a large, glossy card and read, 'A Merry Christmas from The Ideal Tailor, Century Arcade, Star Building, to our esteemed client.' Every year. Never failed. Still had his suits. Snowflakes danced around a Chinese house on stilts. Red Chinese characters and a rosy Father Christmas in the corner.

Suddenly he thought Betty. Longed for Betty. Felt that if he turned round quickly, there she would be. But she was not.

But outside there was a strange sound, a long sliding noise and a thump. A heavy thump. It might well be the taxi skidding on the drive and hitting the house. Filth opened the front door. He saw nothing but snow. He stepped quickly out onto his doorstep for a moment, to look down the drive, and the front door swung to behind him, fastening with a solid, pre-war click.

He was in bedroom slippers. Otherwise he was wearing trousers, a singlet – which he always wore, being a gentleman, thank God – shirt and tie and a thin cashmere cardigan Betty had bought him years ago. It was already sopped through.

Filth walked delicately round the outside of the house, bent forward, screwing up his eyes against the snow, to see if by any chance – but he knew that the back door was locked and all the windows. He turned off towards the tool-shed, over the invisible slippery grass. Locked. He thought of the car in the garage. He hadn't driven it for some time. Mrs Thing did the shopping now. It was scarcely used. But maybe the garage – ? The garage was locked.

Nothing for it but to get somehow down the drive and wait for the taxi under Veneering's yews. On his tiptoe way he passed the heap of snow that had fallen off the roof and sounded like a slithering car. 'Bloody old fool,' said Filth.

At the gate he looked out upon the road. It was a beautiful gleaming sheet of snow in both directions. Nothing had disturbed it for many hours. All was silent as death. Filth turned and looked up at Veneering's drive.

That, too, was untouched, unmarked by birds, un-pocked by falling berries. Snow and snow. Falling and falling. Thick, wet, ice-cold. His bald head, ice-cold. Snow had gathered inside his collar, his cardigan, his slippers. Ice cold. His hands were freezing as he grasped at first one branch and then another of the yews, and, hand over hand, made his way up Veneering's drive.

'He'll have gone to the son,' said Old Filth. 'That or there'll be some house-party going on. Golfers. Smart solicitors.'

But the house was dark and seemed empty, as if it had

been abandoned for years. Old Filth rang the bell and stood in the porch and heard the bell tinkle far away, like Betty's at the rosewood table in the Mid Levels.

'And what the hell do I do next?' he thought. 'He's probably gone to visit that fellow Christopher and they're carousing in the Peninsular. It'll be – what? Late night now. They'll have reached the brandy and cigars and all that vulgarity. Probably kill them. Hello?'

A light had been switched on and a face looked out from a side window. Then the front door opened and a bent old man with a strand or two of still-blond hair peered round it.

'Filth? Come in.'

'Thank you.'

'No coat?'

'I just stepped across. I was looking out for a taxi. For the White Hart. Christmas dinner. Just hanging about. I thought I'd call and –'

'Merry Christmas. Good of you.'

They stood in the drear, un-hollied hall.

'I'll get you a towel. Better take off your cardigan. I'll get you another. Whisky?'

In the brown and freezing sitting-room a huge jigsaw puzzle only one eighth completed was laid out across a table. Table and jigsaw were thick with dust. The venture had a hopeless look. 'Too much damn sky,' said Veneering as they stood looking down at it. 'I'll put another bar on. You must be cold. Maybe we'll hear your cab from here, but I doubt it. I'd guess it won't get through.'

'I wonder if I could use your phone? Mine seems to be defunct.'

'Mine too, I'd guess, if yours is,' said Veneering. 'Try by all means. I scarcely use it.'

The phone was dead.

They sat down before two small red wire-worms of the electric fire. 'Some sort of antique,' thought Filth. 'Haven't seen one in sixty years.' In a display case by the chimney-piece he saw a pair of old exotic earrings. The fire, the earrings, the whisky, the jigsaw, the silence, the eerily-falling snow made him all at once want to weep.

'I was sorry to hear about Betty,' said Veneering.

'I was sorry about Elsie,' said Filth, remembering her name and her still and beautiful Chinese face. 'Is your son – ?'

'Dead,' said Veneering. 'Killed. Army.'

'I am so very sorry. So dreadfully sorry. I hadn't heard.'

'We don't hear much these days, do we? Maybe we did too much hearing. Too many Hearings.'

Filth watched the arthritic, stooped figure shamble across the room to the decanter. 'Not good for the bones, this climate,' said Veneering.

'Did you ever think of staying on?'

'Good God, no.'

'It suited you so well.' Then Filth said something odd. 'Better than us, I always thought. Betty was very Scottish, you know.'

'Plenty of Scots in Hong Kong,' said Veneering. 'You two seemed absolutely welded there. Betty and her Chinese jewellery.'

'Oh, she tried,' said Filth, sadly.

'Another?'

'I should be getting home.'

It dawned on Old Filth that he had not the least idea what was going to happen next. Whatever could happen next? How would this unbelievable visit end?

He would have to ask a favour. A favour of Veneering.

He'd already lost a good point by coming round for help. Veneering was no fool. He'd spotted the dead telephone business. It would be difficult to turn this round – make something of being the first to break the silence. Maturity. Magnanimity. Christmas. Hint of a larger spirit.

He wouldn't mention being locked out. But how would he get home? The cleaning lady's key was three miles away and she wasn't coming in until the New Year. He could hardly stay here – good God, with Veneering!

'I've thought of coming to see you,' said Veneering. 'Several times, as a matter of fact, this past year. Getting on, both of us. Lot of water under the bridge and so on.'

Old Filth was silent. He himself had not thought of doing anything of the sort, and could not pretend. Never could pretend. But he wished now –

'Couldn't think of a good excuse,' said Veneering. 'Bit afraid of the reception. Bloody hot-tempered type I used to be. We weren't exactly similar.'

'I've nearly forgotten what type I was,' said Old Filth, again surprising himself. 'Not much of anything, I expect.'

'Bloody good advocate,' said Veneering.

'I'm told you made a damn good judge,' said Filth, remembering this was true.

'Only excuse I could think of was a feeble one. We've got a key of yours here, hanging in the pantry. Front-door key. Your address on the label. Must have been there for years. Some neighbours being neighbourly long ago I expect. Maybe you have one of mine?'

'No,' said Filth. 'No. I've not seen one.'

'Could have broken in any time,' said Veneering. 'Murdered you in your bed.' There was a flash of the old black mischief. 'Must you go? I don't think there's going to be a taxi. It'll never make the hill. I'll get that key. Unless you want me to hold on to it for an emergency.'

'No,' said Filth. 'I'll take it and see if it works.'

On Veneering's porch, wearing Veneering's (frightful) overcoat, Filth paused. The snow was easing.

He heard himself say, 'Boxing Day tomorrow. If you're on your own I've a ham-shank and some decent claret.'

'Pleasure,' said Veneering.

On his own doorstep Old Filth thought, 'Will it turn?' It did.

His house was beautifully warm but he made up the fire. He started thinking, of all things, about shark's fin soup. There was a tin of it somewhere. And they could have prawns out of the freezer, and rice. Nothing easier. Tin of crab-meat, with the avocado, and parmesan on top. Spot of Soy sauce.

Extraordinary Christmas.

'These are his faults, in no particular order...'

'Martha! How long has this been going on?'

The **Oldie** IN
HOLY MATRIMONY

'Just how pregnant is this pause going to be, Eric?'

'I'm leaving you, dear –
I'll recommend you to one of my friends'

House Husbandry
with Giles Wood

In which Mr Wood finds his patience unaccountably tried by the perfectly pleasant chap next door

'The liberty of the individual must be thus far limited. He must not make himself a nuisance to other people'

JOHN STUART MILL

One million Britons have moved house due to disputes with their neighbours. A forum of thirty thousand, no doubt inspired by the eponymous television programme, has joined a support group called NFHIB (Neighbours from Hell in Britain).

One neighbour in our own terrace seems convivial and harmless to the naked eye but he has become the focus, for me, of what Mary calls an unhealthy obsession.

His predecessors in Number Three were cohabiting New Age dustwomen. Polite and reserved, they sadly moved on when a *feng shui* expert from Glastonbury told them that the ley lines under the cottage were 'toxic'. Next came a blended family who enjoyed impromptu lager garden parties of which, although they inevitably deteriorated into burping competitions, I took an indulgent view. I judged these to fall within the spectrum of traditional English Falstaffian or Chaucerian merrymaking, and to narrowly miss giving grave offence to persons or property.

The same could not be said of the new occupant's wind chimes. They might be appropriate in a Thai massage parlour but with the prevailing westerlies causing them to tinkle inanely 24/7 I now consciously avoid those parts of my garden affected by this pernicious aural pollution.

His almost infinite power to irritate is one that others have recognised in myself

I do not mind that his garden is a tribute in miniature to the Age of Leisure. Gone are the days of airswept lindens yielding their scent; in their place are kebabs and sausages from an almost permanently active ignition barbecue around which folk recline on double hammocks with tassels, or perch on the cedar wishing-well.

But I do mind that he has broken the twenty-year-long village taboo against speaking through the beech hedge. 'Keep at it, Giles!' came his cheery disembodied voice when my toiling Dutch hoe hit a flint. A lesser man might have responded to this attempt at affability but I downed tools and postponed the chore.

Any time I am absent from the village for more than twenty-four hours I am greeted on my return by his beaming face as he mysteriously appears to be always walking his dog while I am parking. 'Hello, stranger!' he quips. 'Been anywhere nice?'

I suspect that the slight curvature of the terraced cottages allows him to watch and wait for my entrances and exits, since every time I unload shopping, or unlock the car in preparation to drive to an appointment, he synchronises his own exits and entrances to ensure maximum entanglement.

'So what else has this friendly fellow done to incur such animosity,' asks Mary, 'when the two of you have so much in common?'

His almost infinite power to irritate is one that others have recognised in myself. He has a lot of time on his hands – this is not the case with me, although I know it is widely believed to be so. We both live in households of demanding women, we both walk dogs of the small spaniel variety, and both our cars are frequently broken down outside the cottages.

'How are you, Giles?' he asked me today as I left the cottage for a routine cholesterol test. It's a question I never like to be asked, especially by someone wearing a compassionate facial expression. 'I don't know,' came my sullen response.

I have come to regard this über-friendly person as a giant human hornet trying to gain access to my house or ingress to my garden. Once he almost outwitted me. 'We've got a good surplus of runner beans here, Giles,' he called through the beech hedge. 'Would you like some?'

Foolishly I said yes, and while I was otherwise engaged he made it through the garden gate and almost into our kitchen before I spotted his game and, blocking his way, ushered him to retreat from whence he came, while accepting his gift of beans.

'Most people can only dream of having friendly neighbours,' says Mary. 'You must be the one exception. But I know why.' Could her attempt at cod psychoanalysis be correct – namely, am I projecting my own shortcomings onto him?

GONE TO POT

Spitting Image puppeteer **ROGER LAW** *experiences the chaotic and occasionally stressful life of a ceramicist in Jingdezhen, China's Porcelain City*

Illustrated by Roger Law

While millions of oldies are muttering about having to work beyond a pensionable age, I decided at the age of seventy to go and work in the sweatshops of Jingdezhen, China's Porcelain City, where porcelain has been made for over a thousand years. And I do mean 'sweatshops'. At times temperatures are above forty degrees with 100 per cent humidity, and sometimes, as a special reward, one returns to the hostel to read the words 'No Water Today'.

If you have no Mandarin, and I don't, to work in Jingdezhen it is essential to find a translator. I found Joey Zhou. Joey turned out to be a humorous and melancholic young man with an insatiable curiosity and a fascination with death. Like everyone in Jingdezhen, Joey makes ceramics. At the time we met he was working on a series of small ceramic gravestones – very ornate with lashings of black and gold. Joey explained that Jingdezhen is not full of huge factories but is made up of hundreds of small family concerns spread throughout the city. Each business specialises to the nth degree and encompasses every kind of ceramic skill you can imagine, from larger-than-life figures of Mao (army coat blown open and arm raised as if hailing a cab in a hurricane) to minute porcelain shirt buttons.

Pots are everywhere. Even the lampposts of Jingdezhen are made of decorated porcelain (peach blossom along one street and dragons down another) which helps to navigate the city, which is exactly what Joey and I did, looking for a place to start work. We would pile into local taxis (mobile adrenalin enhancers), the taxi drivers an aid to Joey's preoccupation with the Reaper. The main roundabout in the city centre sees off citizens on a regular basis, which is just as well, as Joey tells me the ghost of the dead person has to wait until the next fatal accident for a new ghost to replace him. While looking for workshops one morning we spotted a pair of high-heeled shoes, straps buttoned down, standing upright in the middle of the road. We wondered if they belonged to a ghost-in-waiting.

The first workshop Joey and I settled on belonged to Deng Xi Ping. Xi Ping is an important woman in the city with a special stipend from the government to prove it. In her sixties, she is a striking-looking woman with steel-grey hair. I think she took me on because I could afford her prices, and as she had survived the Cultural Revolution she probably thought I would be a walk in the park. We had our ups and downs and some shouting competitions. I sometimes got the feeling she wanted to send me to the countryside for re-education.

I once introduced Deng Xi Ping to a formidable upper-class English woman who declared her to be a proper person. And indeed she is – as professional and reliable as ceramics allow. If you buy one of her pots it is accompanied by a certificate, with a photograph of a much younger Xi Ping, the gold lettering and scarlet binding uncomfortably reminiscent of Mao's 'Little Red Book'.

Deng Xi Ping's spick-and-span factory with its display cases and ordered stock is a far cry from Mr Wu's Big Pot Factory where I work these days. The earth floors are so strewn with debris it is difficult to stand upright. It is also hard to fall down as every inch of space is covered with large pots and young workers painting and carving. The only things sacred are your tools. Step out for a pee and your four-inch stool will be under someone else's bottom on your return. The arguments and teasing among the apprentices make the atmosphere not unlike my old *Spitting Image* workshop.

Pots are everywhere. Even the lampposts of Jingdezhen are made of decorated porcelain – peach blossom along one street and dragons down another

Mr Wu's Big Pots is a bit of an understatement. On my first visit I saw a huge cup and saucer. I climbed into the cup and could only just see over its rim while the accompanying teapot towered above me. I came down with serious pot envy. I had made some small, carved pots with Deng Xi Ping, but now it was clearly time to up the ante.

Most workshops in Jingdezhen are chaotic. In fact everything in this city is filthy except the people. How they achieve this is beyond comprehension. After a day on

the earth floors the men and women emerge spotless, the women's high-heels as clean as the day they were bought from the shop. The potteries ensure plenty of carcinogenic intake – porcelain dust, copper, lead and zinc, glazes and solvents. I bought a pot of glue from an art shop and below the logo were the words in English: 'It is high to glue to fuck the health environmental protection quickly.' No kidding. Refreshingly honest, I thought.

Working at the Big Pot Factory one day I surfaced from drawing the inside of an Ali Baba-sized pot and was waiting for my blood to drain back into place when I noticed someone had left a pair of dirty brown gloves on my sandwiches. The gloves moved. A couple of rats were having an early lunch. Life is hard in the workshops. I am convinced that Kentucky Fried Chicken, known locally as 'The American Embassy', is so popular because it is air-conditioned. When not eating at the Big Pot Factory I can be found in Food Alley which, as the name suggests, is a long and narrow passageway packed with cafés, food stalls and carts. You can down delicious pork and scallion dumplings served in bamboo steamers as you play 'spot the rat' – all frightfully good for the immune system.

Methods of working in Jingdezhen are familiar but I have learned new skills, and with Joey translating I have even been able to show the apprentices a trick or two. Once people realise that you are not there to play, and that you have an understanding of materials and process, a working relationship develops, and the chances are you will be passed from one skilled specialist to another. Joey refrains from translating when a conversation becomes heated – I can become very volatile in 100 per cent humidity. He waits until things calm down. I asked him why the Chinese are not more direct when dealing with problems. 'That is not the Chinese way,' Joey replied sagely. 'They will say nothing and hate you secretly.'

Working in Jingdezhen all adds up to making an old man feel very, very old very, very quickly.

BOX CLEVER

HUBERT GREGG *chaired the Brains Trust in its telly heyday*

No mere B-list celebrities on the BBC sofa in those days: the massed brainpower of (from left to right) A J Ayer, Dr J Bronowski, Robert Bolt, Alan Bullock and Hubert Gregg. Conversation off the set tended to be less weighty…

I n the late Fifties I found myself chairing the television Brains Trust, and oldies abounded. The usual weekly team included Julian Huxley and Dr Bronowski, the hyper-erudite philosopher who some found a touch long-winded; but I suppose if you knew as much as Bronowski you had a right to wind. The rest of them, four in number, were ad hoc choices: Paul Jennings, Marghanita Laski, Alan Bullock et al.

Our schedule was comfortable in the extreme. We would meet for lunch at Scott's at the top of the Haymarket, which it isn't any more. (As the playwright Neil Simon put it, 'If it's old and you like it it won't be there in the morning.') The lunch was cordon bleu, the wine vintage, and so, of course, was the conversation. The producer (whose name now escapes me) and I were hosts and stood by the open door to greet the Brains as they came in. In came Compton Mackenzie – or Monty, as we knew him – and we

shook hands warmly. 'Whom have we with us this week?' he asked, adding, 'Not that little bugger Bronowski, I hope.' 'How do you do?' said a foreign voice behind him.

After lunch our schedule took us by taxi to Lime Grove, which was still a television studio, having once been a film studio. A dummy run for the camera, then to tea and make-up. I had noticed that everyone looked splendid on

'It's the Christian Martyrs' choir…'

camera without make-up. After make-up they lost their natural sheen and became rather puddingy. I pretended to the make-up girl that it gave me dermatitis; I was the only one who looked splendid on camera before and after tea.

H uxley I came to know well. I used to drive him back home to Holland Park after the sessions. He told me of his time at New College with Spooner, and regaled me with tales of the great albino divinity. He said that Spooner didn't make that many spoonerisms as we know them. It is certain that he announced a hymn as 'Cinkering kongs their titles take' and, on finding another sitting in his congregational spot, said, 'Forgive me, sir, but you are occupewing my pie.' But, for the most part, Julian said that Spooner was guilty of what he, Julian, called 'paraphrasia'.

One instance of this occurred when the college was planning a visit to Spitzbergen to see the Northern

Lights. Spooner reported to his wife, 'Do you know, my dear, Huxley tells me the distance from Spitzbergen to the North Pole is no greater than that from Land's End to John of Gaunt.'

My favourite of these tales was of Spooner preaching a lengthy sermon about Aristotle. Julian said he didn't suppose there were more than a handful of people in the congregation who had an informed knowledge of Aristotle, but they gave him a kind of

Some found Dr Bronowski long-winded, but if you knew as much as he did, you had a right to wind

puzzled but rapt attention. Spooner perorated and came to a dramatic finish, then began his way down the spiral staircase. Halfway down he paused, then returned to the pulpit. 'Brethren,' he said, 'in my sermon just now, whenever I mentioned Aristotle, I should have said St Paul.' Satisfied that all was now well, he descended again.

Spooner spent most of his life at New College, as an undergraduate, a Fellow and finally Warden. In this last office he was required to receive Hugh Casson as a new Fellow. Casson arrived and presented himself to Spooner. 'Ah,' said the Warden, 'you must come over to my house for sherry, we're expecting Casson, a new Fellow.' 'But,' said the surprised arrival, 'I'm Casson.' Spooner looked long and hard. 'Never mind,' he said. 'Do come along anyway. I'm sure he'll be delighted to meet you.'

Huxley, I was thrilled to discover, shared my joy at a misprint. And not only a misprint. He told me of the first time the word 'fuck' appeared in a newspaper. It was during the late 19th century, and the newspaper was the *Times*. A sacked linotype operator had his revenge, but only in the first edition.

When Queen Victoria opened a bridge towards the end of the century there appeared – in the *Times* again – the following report. (The second misprint is even more arresting than the first.) 'The ceremony proceeded as though by clockwork. At two-thirty precisely, Her Majesty pissed over the bridge and received an ovation from an enormous crow on the bank.'

ED REARDON'S MONTH

Broadsides from the Bard of Berkhamsted

As told to **ANDREW NICKOLDS**

AM I ALONE in worrying that the rise of the Kindle reading-machine will eventually turn second-hand and remaindered books into endangered species? The damage done to our social history would be incalculable. Though there aren't many crop circles to be seen around now, there are still a number of crop circle picture books, several authored by myself, which may be glimpsed towards the back of shop-windows along the Charing Cross Road. *Helipads of the Gods* is one I remember with particular affection, as the royalties kept me in the lifestyle to which I'd once been accustomed for several months: I'm rather surprised that the groove worn in the pavement between my former house and the Camden Town Oddbins wasn't seized on at the time by the gullible as an inexplicable and probably supernatural phenomenon.

MANY DAILY IRRITATIONS conspire to raise Ed Reardon's blood pressure, starting when I open the wrong end of the packet of blood pressure tablets and am confronted by the folded-up sheet of instructions barring my passage to the medication. Then there is the stressful moment in the supermarket when the PA system crackles into life. Will it be a 'Colleague' or a 'Customer' Announcement? If the former, no problem. But the latter often takes the form of a hapless twelve-year-old doing his or her inadequate best to breathe life into a promotional script for, let us say, half-price ice-cream cones.

There is only one way of avoiding the inevitable horror of the jejune stab at a peroration ('They're brrrrrr-illiant!') and that is to sprint

out of the 'Reduced For Quick Sale' aisle, fingers jammed in ears, and risk colliding with a Shopmobility scooter steered by a speed-crazed pensioner coming in the opposite direction. Weeks spent trying to claim compensation for personal injuries received used to be both a good way to exercise the dramatic muscle and an excellent displacement activity, but now it seems the Legal Aid loophole has closed, rendering litigation an unaffordable pursuit.

But supreme among current bugbears is being talked down to at every turn, as I frequently find myself remarking to Elgar – or 'the legendary Elgar' as I've taken to calling him ever since my cat's namesake was thus described at a recent Prom by some TV newsreader masquerading as a musicologist, who accorded the same 'legendary' status to Delius. Did she assume that I and millions like me tuned in to BBC Two expecting to see *Top Gear* instead, and therefore needed telling that Delius was a legendary composer and not a reasonably priced Peugeot?

IT'S IMPOSSIBLE to change the password to an online poker account without one's head being plunged into a turbid bath of patronising matey-ness from the company's Helpline: 'Whoops! Don't worry!' etc, followed by a 'Nearly there!', and 'Phew!' on completion. I think I shall adopt this strategy when I next need to settle a tax bill. Missed the deadline? 'Oh no! We all do it!' Forgotten to sign the cheque? 'Don't panic – another post-dated one on its way! Please acknowledge receipt by ticking the box marked "Yay!"'

The man who...
also painted pictures

*Artist **LUCY WILLIS** reveals a little-known side of her grandfather,
the famous cartoonist H M Bateman*

My grandfather H M Bateman was one of the most innovative cartoonists of the early 20th century, and as an artist myself I have, for years, pored over his sketch-books and cartoons. But only recently have I really started to appreciate his other work – the serious paintings.

A household name as a cartoonist, he was completely unknown as a painter. But as well as his cartoonist buddies at the London Sketch Club – Heath Robinson, Fougasse and others – he was also friends with such eminent painters as George Clausen, Lucien Pissarro and Philip Connard and had a lifelong ambition to become a 'real artist' like them. At the age of forty, and at the height of his fame, he decided to retire from cartooning and pursue this aim, as he'd hankered to do since his early art school training. He took his painting equipment out into the English countryside and began to travel abroad in search of inspiring subject matter.

A genius in his own field of cartoons he struggled modestly for the rest of his life to master the art of colour and light, continually experimenting with different techniques. It's extraordinary that a man who had expressed such extremes of emotion, even violence, in his use of line could produce paintings of such gentle serenity as *Fishing Boats, Mgarr.*

When I decided to go and paint in Malta and Gozo in 2011 I had a strong ulterior motive: Grandpa had spent his last five years there and I had recently come across a number of his paintings of the islands, unspoilt as they were in the late 1960s. The pictures were unsigned, undated and gave no hint of location. Clearly he had little or no expectation of them ever being exhibited.

I planned to identify the specific scenes he had painted and to see how they looked now – maybe paint them myself. It involved considerable sleuth work but I was aided and abetted by some very enthusiastic Maltese and Gozitans. The folder of images I took with me was passed from hand to hand until someone, with delight,

THE COLONEL IMPLORES HIS DAUGHTER TO BE REASONABLE.

recognised the view in question.

Early on my first morning in Gozo I climbed the steps behind the hotel, built on the site of the Royal Lady Hotel where my grandfather had lived out his days. There I saw a man mending fishing nets, sitting on the ground exactly as Grandpa had

painted fishermen forty years before. I asked if he had, by any chance, known an elderly English painter, seen about Mgarr in the late 1960s. He thought not, but then something jogged his memory. At the age of fourteen, he said, he had been walking home one evening when he came across the body of a man with a little white beard, lying in the lane. We have always known that my grandfather had died peacefully, aged 82, while out walking.

It was an extraordinary discovery to make within hours of setting foot on the island. The fisherman showed me the view of St Anthony's Church from his roof, exactly as Grandpa had painted it from the roof of the Royal Lady. I met others who had known him – boat-builders who had chatted to him on his daily painting excursions; his doctor who recalled the impromptu cartoon of the two of them, drawn on his prescription pad. Most rewarding of all was the response to the paintings themselves, which have been hailed in Valetta as a rare and precious record of a bygone era on the islands: the brightly coloured houses, the fleets of extravagantly painted fishing boats and the donkey carts – now nearly all of them gone.

At the height of his fame, Bateman decided to retire from cartooning and pursue painting, as he'd hankered to do since his early art school training

GRANNY ANNEXE

Virginia Ironside

Day-tripper

Memory lane. It's a road that only old people can walk down, isn't it? I mean young people can of course walk down theirs if they wish, but they've barely taken a single stride before they've hit the maternity ward and, before that, their mother's womb. Their memory lanes are exceedingly short – like tiny alleys – while old people's memory lanes stretch back and back, like the M1. I gather that those who are kidnapped or taken hostage often while away the hours by walking, in their minds, down their own memory lanes, which is why, presumably, it's so much easier being a hostage when you're past middle age than it is when you're young – a lot more to think about.

Of course when you walk down your own memory lane there are vast swathes of it that are completely unmemorable, rather like the stretch of the M4 from Heathrow to Bristol – miles and miles of nothingness. But there are bits that start out at you, like the glimpse of Stonehenge from the A303, or the sighting of the Angel of the North on the A1. And nothing has quite such poignant resonance than those very early bits, when we were growing up, when all our experiences were the first, and all our visual images had never been seen before.

I've often wondered why I have such a penchant for wartime London. I love the books of Julian Maclaren-Ross, his descriptions of ill-lit pubs, the foggy, badly-lit London streets, the bombed-out

Sheppey was the landscape of my youth, with burnt-out churches and belching chimneys

Kensington squares, the faulty geysers and the smell of people's sweat and unwashed hair. I now realise it's because, grisly and unprepossessing as they are, they remind me of my childhood.

Recently I went to the Isle of Sheppey. I had no idea what drew me there, but the moment I arrived I recognised it at once. It was the landscape of my youth, with burnt-out churches, belching chimneys from industrial works, lack of planning, peeling houses and vast stretches of scrubby wasteland, punctuated by cranes and pylons, thin and cowering dogs, all unloved, decayed and slightly hostile. There were even houses with tattered Union Jacks outside. Everything looked so out of the Fifties that I was expecting to see boarding houses with notices on their front doors proclaiming 'No Blacks or Irish, please'.

Friends were astonished that I wanted to make a day trip there. Why not go to Blenheim Palace or Brighton Pavilion – places bursting with historical interest

and brilliantly spiffed up with English Heritage or National Trust money? But there's no atmosphere in, and more importantly, no connection with, those polished rooms, their over-stuffed chairs marred by a single fir-cone signalling, in an ever-so-polite way, that they're not for sitting on, their ropes that make you feel completely alienated from the space.

In Sheppey I had one of the most enjoyable days of my life. 'Let's go when it's freezing and miserable,' said my friend when we were plotting the trip. 'It wouldn't be so good on a sunny day.' And he was right. To get fully into the spirit of things we ate, before visiting Sheerness Prison (a more desolate place than any I have ever seen), the most disgusting fish and roe and chips in the car.

We're planning a trip to the dank and decaying world of St Leonards-on-Sea. After that, to Margate, where the skeleton of a ghostly fairground big dipper still survives where the old funfair used to be, and finally there's Clacton-on-Sea, which, I'm told, is full of boarded-up old grand hotels.

It's an odd sort of sightseeing, I know. But it's my personal memory lane. And I'm already wondering if my grandchildren, faced with travelling down their own memory lanes when they're in their sixties, won't find that visiting shopping malls and eating long out-of-date burgers will fill them not only with horror but also a weird sort of nostalgia – and, indeed, comfort.

Just the same feeling as I got from my strange trip to Sheppey.

Rack my brains as I might, I cannot think of any benefit I have ever received as a result of the existence of the monarchy, nor can I think of any benefit or favour I am ever likely to receive, or any of my friends or relations is likely to receive, from the existence of the royal family.

Having said all that, I must also admit that neither the monarchy nor any member of the royal family has ever done me any harm. They may have constructed a high wall around themselves to keep me out, but I am quite happy to be excluded, and have no desire to hobnob with those on the other side of the wall. There are people who can whip up a sense of grievance at being excluded from what may seem to be a charmed circle, dedicated to celebrating its own unearned privileges, but these people should be required to submit to counselling, rather than encouraged. Practically everybody in Britain is at the receiving end of some 200 years' accumulated rights and privileges which they have done nothing to deserve. As the Reverend J C Flannel might point out, we are not starving to death as they are in Somalia, but on top of these negative advantages we have inherited a whole battery of privileges which put the British, through no virtue or effort of their own, but only through the efforts of their ancestors, among the ten luckiest nations of the world. Our whole existence is a celebration of unearned privilege. We are on a very weak wicket if we devote ourselves to envying each other, but if ever envious hatreds are allowed to prevail, and to become a dominant force in society, the entire basis of our comfort and prosperity will collapse. Perhaps one cannot expect those journalists who cry for the monarchy to be abolished to have read Simon Schama's brilliant account of the subsequent history of the French Revolution, *Citizens*, let alone to have studied the history of the Bolshevik revolution in Russia, but we already have the same sequence laid out before our gaze in the British press. In the van we have the delicate twitterings of fun-republicans; in the middle of the column we have angrier *ad hominem* (or, more accurately, *ad mulierem*) attacks. Many are intelligent and witty writers, whose hearts are generally in the right place. The shame is that they do not pause to

AUBERON WAUGH

look over their shoulders to see what is bringing up the rear of their brave little forays into enemy territory: the great grumbling, groaning ranks of professional malcontents, psychopaths eaten up by hatred of anyone who is successful or lucky or attractive or care-free; woman-haters, haters of children and old people and Pekingeses, anti-hunting, anti-smoking, anti-drinking, anti-driving, anti-Europe, anti-eating, expecting out of life nothing more than to sit watching rotten American films supplied by satellite or cable television: classless, sexless, odourless – in a phrase, the Murdoch New Brit. If ever the Murdoch New Brit takes over this country, we might as well all go and live in Afghanistan.

'She's shy with strangers'

Even without the spectre of Murdoch and his cringing thugs, there are good reasons why we should distance ourselves from the move to get rid of the monarchy. If I pinch myself, I can think of good reasons for retaining the whole circus; it causes great pleasure to an enormous number of people as the Queen goes round patting dim, meritorious people on the back, and does no harm to anybody; it amuses and stimulates the whole country, and gives us something to talk about which is more interesting than the weather, less unpleasant than sport. Anybody who has visited Vienna since the Habsburgs were kicked out will see how much dimmer and dingier London will become if its royal palaces are turned into museums, and its royal elevations and avenues and enfilades serve no further purpose.

The chief reason for getting rid of the monarchy might be for the rancour and cruelty it excites, which sometimes give the impression that we are not a nation of human beings at all. Even those of us who smiled at the exposure of the Duchess of York as a selfish, empty-headed vulgarian might have been alarmed at the hounding of the Princess of Wales (who may or may not have set the pack on her husband first – none of us knows for sure). But the public debate on whether or not she had ever had carnal relations with James Gilbey, or Major Hewitt, or anyone else, is so vilely insulting to everybody concerned that it diminishes us all.

Or so I would maintain. But even if I am right, the same pack will set upon someone else with the same degree of sadism as soon as it has destroyed the monarchy. The chief reason for keeping the monarchy is that it happens to be there. The old have always been criticised for their conservatism, but it is not really a criticism so much as a tautology. It is an essential part of existence that every-thing (except God, if you like) eventually deteriorates; as familiar things deteriorate, they are replaced by the unfamiliar. Part of our rage against the dying of the light must be directed towards propping up what is old and decrepit and falling to pieces, resisting what is new and unfamiliar. It is only through a sense of historical continuity that we can keep sane in the post-religious age. Out with Murdoch and God save the Queen.

27

Look back *in affection*

The young John Osborne made costume designer **JOCELYN RICKARDS** *laugh, and very soon joined her long list of lovers...*

In 1958 I had already been working for some weeks on the film of *Look Back in Anger* when John Osborne and Mary Ure returned from New York, where Mary had been starring as Alison, the put-upon wife in the play's Broadway production. Harry Saltzman, a wheeler-dealing Canadian, was to produce the film. He'd taken a small house in Belgravia, and it was into this house that John and Mary exploded.

Despite the short duration of their marriage – eleven months – neither had been faithful during their New York sojourn: Mary had had an affair with the actor Robert Webber, and John a liaison with a beautiful upmarket hooker introduced to him by Saltzman. But of this I had no knowledge that first evening when, fizzing like champagne cocktails, they overflowed into Lowndes Cottage, presenting an image of dazzling glamour – Mary milk-pale with her ashy blonde head rising like a flower from the scooped neck of her Mary Quant dark brown suede dress, and John thin, elegant and very sunburnt, wearing a pink denim shirt and a pair of khaki trousers. His blue eyes, like small chips of sapphires, blazed from his brown face.

Mary Ure was John's second wife, and he treated her with derision. They had married after being caught up in the electrifying success of *Look Back in Anger*, and then seemed not to know what to do with each other. All his life, John retained a residual feeling for his first wife, Pamela Lane, scurrying off to keep assignations with her.

I was underwhelmed when we first met. I moved in a world peopled by older writers, intellectuals and – God forbid that I now write it – 'patricians'. I wasn't about to be swept off my feet by a young actor turned playwright, no matter how successful. I liked them both and got to know them slowly, but it was not until the next year, when working with John on *The World of Paul Slickey*,

that I found myself becoming attracted to him. We worked with the architect Hugh Casson and the choreographer Kenneth MacMillan, both of whom I had introduced to John.

On the night of the last pea-soup fog I can remember, John, Kenneth

He was six years younger than I, who had never had a younger lover before. Whoopee!

and I had dinner together and went back afterwards to Woodfall Street, John's bijou house off the King's Road. Sometime after midnight Kenneth and I opened the front door to leave and were beaten back by an invasive waft of stinking, yellow murk. We tried telephoning the taxi rank – nothing. I said, 'I'm *not* walking home in that,' and John replied, 'And I'm not driving you.' Eventually Kenneth elected to grope his way blindly, and John and I were left alone together. Mary was in Stratford-upon-Avon rehearsing, and there was no spare bed, so *faute de mieux* we became lovers, and liked

'I've had enough of character building, Dad. Can I support a successful team now?'

it. My only reservations were about Mary's frilled, lilac sheets. It was like being wrapped in some giant's nightie.

Initially, the only person who knew about our fall from grace was Alec Murray, the photographer, with whom I shared a flat in Eaton Square. When I returned in the morning he eyed me bleakly and said, 'Oh Jocelyn, you fucking fool.'

'Don't nag, Alec. I don't feel particularly wise, but no one's going to get hurt.'

Alec and I had known each other since I was fourteen, and at twenty I had made him a present of my unwanted virginity. By now we were each other's closest friend.

I seriously considered my position with John. I did not want to marry him. I enjoyed him, he made me laugh, so I would disengage myself from the incumbent lover (Wolf Mankowitz) and see what happened.

What happened? I fell in love with him – head over heels. He was six years younger than I, who had never had a younger lover before. Whoopee!

In those early days John was a nut cutlet vegetarian. He drank only beer and Scotch and puffed enthusiastically on a pipe loaded with a sweet-scented American tobacco bought from a tobacconist in Sloane Square. We worked on *Paul Slickey* on tour until its opening in London at the Prince's Theatre, Cambridge Circus. It was a flop of unbelievable dimensions. At 26 John had created a furore with his first play, and consolidated his position with *The Entertainer* for Laurence Olivier. *Slickey* was his first disaster. The audience booed, the gossip columnists howled with grim pleasure and the critics dismissed it more in sorrow than in anger.

As the tumult and shouting diminished to a weary hoot, John and I packed ourselves into his new racing-green convertible Jaguar and set off on holiday. We arranged to meet Alec in

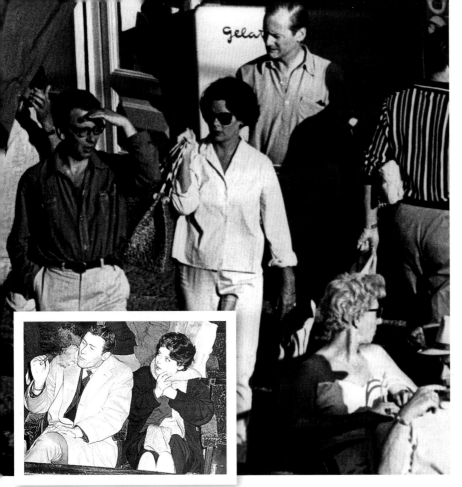

A paparazzi shot of Jocelyn Rickards with Alec Murray when they were holidaying with John Osborne in the Bay of Naples, 1959
Inset: Jocelyn and John in 1959

Rome and drove along the secondary roads of France. John learned to drink wine instead of beer and to eat food rather than nut cutlets. It was a time of relaxation and affirmation, and an amazingly perfect holiday. In Rome we met Alec, who was full of gloomy stories in the national press about husbands holidaying apart from their wives. 'You know there's a trail of agency photographers on your tail.' We had no idea. John and Alec became close friends and John said of him one day, 'He's the only aristocrat I have ever met.'

With Alec fitted snugly into the back of the Jaguar, we sped along the autostrada to Naples, a fine rain bringing out the scents of the Italian countryside. We spent the night in Naples, and left next morning for Capri. On arrival we took a taxi to the summit of the island, up as far as we could go, to Caprile; then we walked along a footpath until we reached the high white wall and secure iron gate of the Villa Rosario, which Graham Greene had lent me. Inside the wall, the Bay of Naples spread out in front of us – and with the gate locked, we were safe from marauding newspaper stringers. We eluded them until the last evening when, running to catch a taxi, they caught up with the reprehensible sinning lovers. Back in London, both Eaton Square and Woodfall Street were staked out by men in grubby raincoats and grimy felt hats, notebooks at the ready. I escaped, but John was trapped between the front door and the end of the cul-de-sac.

The affair continued like a rollercoaster. John was anxious to get me into some kind of privacy. His solicitor found us the top three and a half floors of a house in Lower Belgrave Street, and I moved in my paints, easels and reference books. Alec was the only person welcome at all times, using his own idiosyncratic ring to gain admission. Boxing and coxing, John continued to return to Woodfall Street each night.

He desperately wanted a child, and – not without difficulty – I eventually conceived with the help of a fertility specialist recommended by Barbara Skelton. With me safely pregnant, John decided to go to LA to see Tony Richardson and Mary Ure, who was appearing with Vivien Leigh in *Duel of Angels*. I miscarried at the end of the third month. John left Mary in San Francisco; we met in Paris, and returned to Lower Belgrave Street for the only truly peaceful time we ever spent.

One day John announced that he was so jealous of himself that he never felt jealousy for anyone else – whatever that may have meant. I think he was seriously miffed about Mary and Robert Webber, and he was jealous of both Freddie Ayer, whom he purported to despise, and Graham Greene: one evening he stormed out of the theatre in the interval of a play of Graham's saying, 'I don't have to stay and watch this rubbish.' I could have killed him. He certainly felt jealousy about Jocelyn Herbert, whose only crime was to love and be loved by George Devine, who remained a hero to John all his life. He refused to see either her charm or the imaginative skill in the work she did in the theatre. I found his attitude to women immature. I don't think he much liked them, and fidelity was totally beyond his ken – except with Jill Bennett, with whom he was sexually obsessed before and during their marriage. All the rest of his wives and I were cast aside, like so many old socks with holes in them.

The wimpish Madeleine Carroll as the Princess Flavia in the film of *The Prisoner of Zenda* was his idea of the most desirable woman in the world. The only one of his ladies who even remotely resembled her was Mary – but that was only physical. When he wasn't mooning after Flavia he had endless fantasies about red hair and schoolgirls' knickers – neither of which I could share with him.

Mary Ure returned from California and John returned to the marital bed. Some months later they were woken in the middle of the night by flames licking through Woodfall Street. After being carried to safety by firemen, Mary was taken to a hotel, while John turned up, covered in soot, at Lower Belgrave Street around four a.m. It was the end of their marriage. Mary was pregnant by Robert Shaw.

In 1961 John eventually went off with Penelope Gilliatt to a house I had chosen and loved in Sussex, with the River Cuckmere looping through the garden. Penelope defiled it with white wall-to-wall carpeting. She was the most intellectually pretentious woman I have ever met, but her hair was like a burning bush and she would don gym slips, nurses' uniforms and schoolgirls' knickers for John's delectation. It didn't do her any good. That marriage foundered, and he moved on to wives four and five. We continued to meet for dinner and talk on the telephone, and when he died I grieved – but I see him now as a flawed and disappointed man, who just occasionally wrote like an angel.

GETTING IN TOUCH
WITH THE PUBLISHER WITHIN

SUSAN HILL *thought she was a writer. Then she discovered bubblewrap...*
Before self-publishing became popular, she had begun her own business

Inside each of us, someone different is trying to get out. I think we should encourage it, if only because, as Roy Strong says, the way to stay young is to have a new career every ten years.

I am a writer, but inside there's a market trader. It's inherited. My mother ran a small company manufacturing children's clothes, and designed and hand-made posh frocks for Yorkshire ladies. I grew up surrounded by pins, patterns and pinking shears, and sat under sewing machines reading. For, to my mother's chagrin, I was bookish, the only child in the handicraft class whose hemming had to be unpicked four times. But I loved the workrooms and, even more, the business parapher-nalia, the order and invoice books, with their flimsy blue carbon inserts, the ready reckoner and the appointments diary, the packing room, with its huge rolls of brown paper and tissue.

But the embryo businesswoman got buried under the books – though when I came to write them, I followed their progress eagerly from manuscript to shop, taking in printers and bindery on the way. Something stirred when I read about my heroine, the Duchess of Devon-shire, starting a successful farm shop at Chatsworth. There she was, I thought admiringly, just making good use of what she found in the larder at the time. Then I found something in my own larder. Between novels, I always used to write short stories. Then I stopped. Odd how these things come and go. But, after a life and near-death crisis in 1995, four stories surfaced from my sub-conscious, or larder; not enough for my usual publishers to make into a full-length book, so I was about to shove them into a drawer, when I chanced to read, in

Virginia Woolf's diary: 'We have printed off the text of "Kew Gardens" and got an estimate from McDermott for printing Murry's poems... We supply the paper and cover. Possibilities are opened up, I think.' Possibilities indeed. If she, my other heroine, a genius of a writer, could also help run the Hogarth Press, be a publisher, even to the extent of doing some printing... No sooner was the thought thought, than I had decided. I was going to be a publisher, beginning with my own new stories.

I phoned some friends in the trade and discovered that it would make perfect economic sense to do a small-format paperback. In one bound, the businesswoman was free. That night, I looked across the garden at the long stone barn, in the converted granary loft of which I work. 'Long Barn Books,' I said.

Next day, I read in Virginia Woolf's diary: 'Just back from three days with Vita, at Long Barn.' As my mother would have said through a mouthful of pins, 'It was meant'.

Which is how I found myself returning from taking my daughter to riding, one August morning, shopping bags full of dog biscuits and cabbages, to grab the ringing telephone in the kitchen, remembering in time to say: 'Long Barn Books, good morning.'

'This is the XYZ Bookshop here. I'd like to order twenty copies of Susan Hill's *Listening to the Orchestra*, please.'

Drop carrier bags. Search for pen. Where do kitchen pens go? 'Would you just bear with me a moment?' (Well, all telesales girls say that.) Race upstairs. Find pen and order book. Race down

again. But now the bookseller wants the book's ISBN number. ISBNs are not memorable and that file is at the top of the house. Race up. Get number. Race down. Hear kettle boiling over below. Race further down. Remove kettle. Race back. Give ISBN to nice bookseller, who then asks, terribly politely, if there might be any chance of speaking to me, as it were.

'You are. This is. I am me.'

'But how extraordinary.'

'I'm sorry?'

'I imagined there was a staff of twenty... not just you, running up and down stairs.'

But so much is it just me running up and down stairs that my daughter invented a telephone routine for me:

'"Good morning, Long Barn Books, which department – Management, Editorial, Production, Design, Accounts, Publicity, Sales and Marketing, Post Room or Canteen?" It'll all be you, Mummy, but they're not to know that.'

Being a small publisher is altogether delightful. It is also remarkably straightforward and I have demystified a lot of things, though it helps to have been in the book world for so long and know such a lot of helpful people. I don't have to print myself off the kitchen table either, like the Woolfs, though in some ways I wish I did. The new technology has made my new career possible.

I am still a writer first. I go alone, into the silence of the Long Barn, to work on a new novel, which I won't be publishing myself. But, back in the house for coffee, I can't resist running up to check the fax machine for orders.

I wonder if Virginia Woolf ran up and down stairs all day... I wonder if the Duchess of Devonshire does... (some stairs)... Virginia Woolf called the Hogarth Press a hobby... I bet the D of D doesn't say that of Chatsworth... Virginia Woolf wouldn't have said 'bear with me' either... I have negotiated a further five per cent discount on bubblewrap... the Long Barn is full of books... and bubblewrap... I have finished another chapter of the novel... I am quite pleased with it... I have to go now, to fetch my daughter from riding...'Good afternoon, Long Barn Books ...'

Here comes a van, laden with bubblewrap... Help... inside this writer was a publisher who just got out... Inside this... ?

Notes from the sofa
Briggs the tea-leaf

Written and illustrated by **RAYMOND BRIGGS**

I AM A CRIMINAL, a common thief. I have three confessions to make.

ONE: Every week I get two breaded lemon soles from Waitrose. These delicate items are packed extra carefully into the correct Waitrose cool bag.

One week, they were so carefully packed I didn't find them until I opened our fridge at home. Oh dear... don't remember these at the checkout... hastily dug out receipt... no fish on it.

What do I do? Phone them? Drive five miles back? Forget it? 'That which is done cannot be undone.' Not without a lot of fiddle-arse anyway. Forget it.

TWO: Last autumn I saw an advertisement for a crate of wine. It sounded good, also amazingly cheap. I thought: 'I might send for that...'

A few days later, I came home to find a large cardboard box on the step. Puzzled, I dragged it indoors and opened it. Wine! That box I was going to order... did I do it? Can't remember... must have done... the aged brain.

So easy nowadays – phone up, name, postcode, card number... all done in a couple of minutes. Of course you can forget.

A few days later, came home, *another* box on the step exactly like the first one. Address on top said Ivy Cottage, just up the lane. What a coincidence, they ordered the same wine as me! Gave them a ring, they said they would collect, which they did, though I never saw them.

A few weeks later, when my box was empty, I was dumping it by the bin. It rolled over and there on the bottom was a label: Ivy Cottage. Oh, dear. 'That which is done...'

THREE: At the Queen's birthday garden party we were all drinking champagne in the Palace and were then ushered into the garden. I was still holding a full glass and when it was empty I looked for somewhere to put it down, but there was nowhere except the lawn itself.

Just then, we were rounded up to be presented to Her Majesty and I realised I could not shake hands with the Queen whilst holding a glass in the other hand, so I hurriedly thrust it into my jacket pocket. Later, half asleep on the train, there was something prodding into my side. I felt into a pocket and took out the glass, engraved with the Royal Coat of Arms. Oh dear.

So I have stolen from Waitrose, defrauded a wine merchant and robbed Her Majesty the Queen.

For once I don't blame the parents. I do blame the school, which was a so-called grammar school in South London called Rutlish.

A pupil there a few years before me was one George Neville Heath, who oldies will remember was a sadistic serial killer of women; hanged, of course. Then, a few years after me, came someone called John Major, a one-time Prime Minister, not hanged.

With a background like that, what hope have I?

Whiteboard *jungle*

KATE SAWYER

The art of euphemism

When I was a child, reports came once a year, in the summer, in a mysterious brown envelope. Feeling faintly sick, I would carry them home to my mother who would read them in silence, leaving me to gauge her reaction by her facial expressions.

Of course I never considered the writing of the reports, never (I must have been very stupid) thought about how many times the wretched teacher had to write 'could do better' before she could reach wearily for her glass of wine.

Many teachers complain bitterly about report writing, but I have to admit to finding a perverse satisfaction in the job. The first set of reports I had to write was for a Year II girl group I had inherited from an embittered male teacher. I had nightmares about them, would have to force myself, trembling, through the door every time they were timetabled. I never cried in front of them, but it was a close-run thing. They were a pack, hunting me with an unerring instinct as to how to cause pain.

And then came my revenge. The reports.

In those days the reports were left in the staff room, and teachers had to queue to take their turn to handwrite them. I have seen some bitter scuffles break out over whose turn it was to take the stack. 'Can I put "Your daughter is an idle slag"?' I asked my head of department, all wide-eyed innocence. His look of panic was almost worth the six months of misery the girls had given me. Then I wrote, 'Had I seen as much of your daughter's work as I have of the inside of her makeup bag, I would be in more of a position

> '*Can I put "Your daughter is an idle slag"?' I asked my head of department, all wide-eyed innocence*

to judge her chances of success in the summer.' To anyone who can read between the lines, that clearly said 'Your daughter is an idle slag.'

And that is the joy of report writing. It brings the art of euphemism to a new high. In a few words you can praise or denigrate, mock or massacre, in the sad knowledge that at least half the parents won't pick up the subtleties or even care. Sometimes it backfires. When I wrote, 'Had I been looking for a drummer for my swing band, I would have fallen upon your son with cries of joy' to the parents of a boy whose obsessive drumming on the desk had nearly

driven me to violence – they actually rang the school to ask if their son could audition for the band.

Now that reports are all written on line, many teachers cut and paste. I suppose it's easier but it takes all the fun out of it and also lays the teachers open to hideous mistakes with names and even sexes. The drama teacher has two reports: 'X plays a full part in drama' and 'Y does not have the maturity to perform seriously or satisfactorily.' Now where's the fun in that?

'Z is a polite girl. She is always conscientious but could contribute more in class' means that the teacher can't actually remember who Z is. On other hand 'P is very quick to volunteer' means she's an infuriating goody goody and you wish she'd occasionally shut up.

There's another whole sub-plot to reports, of course. If the parents knew how many teachers' reports have to be corrected for spelling, apostrophes and even basic grammar they would rightly be horrified.

But that is a whole different story...

'...and so we say goodbye to Stanley, perhaps not the most popular of men'

Montmartre

*If you're looking for romantic Parisian atmosphere, stay well clear
of the 18ème, warns* **SONALI CHAPMAN**

Today Montmartre, the 18th arrondissement in the north of Paris, has the reputation of being a romantic centre of the arts – thronging with writers and cabaret artists, the charm of the *Belle Epoque* still lingering in the air. In reality, nothing could be further from the truth. Nobody can deny the beauty of the Basilique du Sacré-Coeur, but perhaps the reason it was originally built set the future tone of the area.

Construction of the basilica began in the 1870s, during the tumultuous period after the 1870 defeat by the Prussians and the ensuing uprising of the Paris Commune – and was the result of the National Vow made in 1873 to atone for the lack of religious faith in the city, and 'to expiate the crimes of the Communards'. In other words, the Roman Catholic basilica became for many Parisians a symbol of repression. Today, it's the focal point of the *quartier*, crowning the Butte Montmartre, and is visited by thousands of tourists each year, many of whom have no understanding of its place in Parisian history.

In fact, a sense of history in this *quartier* has gone altogether rather awry. Stretching away from the basilica down the hill towards the Rue des Abbesses, in the ancient maze of streets, is a plethora of overpriced cafés and coffee shops in an assumed and overtly 'Parisian' style. They are the kind of cafés a tourist would *expect* to see in Paris, though very few Parisians can actually be seen drinking there. The effect of these establishments, crammed together, their tables and chairs spilling onto the cobbles, surrounded by shops selling tat (Eiffel Tower fridge magnets and reproduction art nouveau postcards) is rather that of a 'Paris-themed area' in a Disney or Las Vegas theme park. In fact, if this is all you see of Paris, you'd be better off going to Las Vegas instead.

Montmartre isn't any more real.

The Cimetière de Montmartre isn't far away, of course, and this is certainly worth a visit (perhaps the only remnant of the truly romantic in the area), but around every corner you'll find a tourist looking for the grocery shop used in the film *Amélie*. The shop has now plastered its windows with newspaper cuttings, and sells more photographs of its façade than it sells fruit. Close by – and next stop on

> ### If this is all you see of Paris you'd be better off going to Disney or Las Vegas. Montmartre isn't any more real

the tourist trail – is the Moulin Rouge on the Boulevard de Clichy, a fifteen-minute walk downhill through cluttered streets lined with shops selling cheap clothes. This Parisian 'legend' is actually a nondescript, tacky – and tiny – 'windmill' covered in neon flashing lights and surrounded entirely by coach parties of (mainly American) tourists taking photographs of each other, the girls wearing only their bras in an effort to look like 'courtesans'. In front of the Moulin Rouge is a chaotic death-trap of a roundabout. Cross the road at your peril: you won't be able to get through the coaches or taxis to the other side.

The *pièce de résistance*, however, is the view, immediately apparent, of the seedy Parisian sex scene, stretching away in all its glory down the boulevard on either side of the Moulin Rouge. The clubs, brothels and sex shops, run by owners willing to exploit the trade of human trafficking for a tidy sum, are exceedingly depressing – and feel endless.

Burlesque? You won't find that here any more. Romantic? My *derrière*...

Dea's bee catastrophe

In the mangrove swamps of Costa Rica **DEA BIRKETT**
came face to face with the stuff of science fiction...

We were gliding up the mangrove swamp. Huge white herons landed only feet away from us, and a crab-eating buzzard with a stout hooked beak for cracking open the shells rested on a branch above. 'We couldn't get within fifty metres of these anywhere else in the world,' said Eckhard, our guide. But this was the tiny Central American country of Costa Rica, where wildlife comes so close it can almost peck you. Toads as big as dinner plates burped in our face. Tiny black crabs scuttled along the twisted mangrove trunks. It's a sad reflection on my home life, but at first I thought the different bird songs were so many mobile phones going off in the jungle. My boyfriend, my six-year-old daughter and I were being taken through the tributaries of the Rio Nosara, a broad mangrove creek on Costa Rica's Pacific coast. Eckhard, in his fifties, was as brown as a date, wearing a Panama hat, reef sandals and a beard. He'd been a printer in his native Germany but now

lived in a *rancho* – a traditional circular house built from tree trunks with a palm-frond roof – near Nosara, where he worked as a naturalist. He guided us through the tangled tributaries in his tiny aluminium boat with a small electric engine powered by a car battery, so it was almost silent.

Eckhard pointed out the bank of sand where the alligators lie in the sun, the shape of their three-metre-long bodies still clearly imprinted like giant footprints. It has never been known for an alligator to attack someone, and the local villagers go safely snorkelling for shrimps up the same saltwater creeks. There was just a whisper of danger, enough to make the nerves tingle pleasantly, but nothing threatening at all. Or so we thought.

For a nanosecond, I presumed it was just another fly bothering me. Then Eckhard screamed, 'Don't move!

Don't move!' They descended upon us, smothering our skin until it was all bumpy and black. They were everywhere, and all Eckhard kept shouting was, 'Don't move! Don't move!' I threw myself over my daughter like a blanket of flesh and bone, closed my eyes and prayed. The worst thing was the noise, a ceaseless drone so loud and so close it seemed almost to be coming from under, not on, our skin. We were being attacked by a swarm of killer bees.

> *The worst thing was the noise, a ceaseless drone so loud and so close it seemed almost to be coming from under, not on, our skin. We were being attacked*

My boyfriend was the first to be stung. He lashed out, instinctively brushing the bee from his forearm. That was a mistake. A killer bee regards any sign of movement as an act of aggression. Like some Hitchcock nightmare, the bees retaliated, and he was stung again. But Eckhard was attacked the worst. With his head up, trying to steer the boat away from the swarm as quickly as possible, they went for his uncovered face. The stings first broke like little splinters, quickly becoming craters of red. His eyes swelled up, then he ballooned around his ears and neck. I thought, peeping out, if Eckhard – an old hand at jungle treks – thinks this is OK, we'll be OK. But Eckhard was shaking. His hand wobbled on the tiller so much he could barely steer. I offered to take his place, but I had no idea where the twisted roots of the mangrove trees lay under the shallow creek and couldn't have navigated our way through the maze of tributaries back to the broad brown Rio Nosara, our highway home.

We couldn't shake the bees off. They followed us down the tributary, encircling Eckhard. I glanced back again; his Panama hat was like an umbrella of bees. 'They're still on me, aren't they?' he groaned, too terrified to move his head or flick his hands to check himself. 'Yes,' was all I said, with a mouth as tight as a ventriloquist's.

They weren't only on him, they were in him – inside his ears and up his nostrils. I couldn't help. I could barely watch, so frightened was I that if I lifted my head they might go for my face, too. And I couldn't offer to brush them off, as they would just bite right back. When killer bees attack, you have to somehow try to escape.

After many long minutes, our tiny battery-powered boat began to outrun the bees. A few stragglers hung on, determined to punish us for invading their untamed territory. As we puttered back, past the place where the alligators sun, we said nothing except a quiet chorus of, 'You all right? You all right?' Eckhard had fifteen bites and was feeling quite woozy. My boyfriend had just two, my daughter one. I was the only one to escape unbitten.

Despite rumours to the contrary, attacks like this are unusual. In eight years as a guide in Costa Rica, Eckhard had only been attacked once before, four years previously. On that occasion, bitten 25 times, he had been fortunate to have been taking a doctor down the creek. They went ashore on the bank where the alligators sun (all danger is relative), where the doctor put his feet up so blood went to his heart.

Bees are not native to Central America. In 1956, African honey-bees – *Apis mellifera scutellata* – were imported from Tanzania to Brazil, where the introduction of the European honey-bee had not been entirely successful. The Africans were more aggressive but used to hot weather, and produced five times as much honey as the Europeans. South American scientists wanted to breed a higher-producing honey-bee suited to the climate. But then the science fiction story began. In 1957 26 colonies of African bees escaped from a research apiary in Brazil and mated with the more docile Europeans. Their progeny began to spread throughout South and Central America. This new strain was different from its parents, but not as hoped. The Africanised honey-bee, soon known as the killer bee, is smaller, more vigorous and swarms more often. It stings up to ten times more than the European bee. It defends its hive more quickly and pursues intruders greater distances, sometimes up to half a mile. In technical language, killer bees have an 'excessive level of colony defence'. They sting when you invade their territory, though how you can recognise the true borders of killer-bee land on a Costa Rican creek is a mystery not even Eckhard could unfold.

The number of recorded deaths from attacks by killer bees is sometimes given as twenty, sometimes over a thousand. Almost all of these are in Central and South America. But it was only when the bees began marching north that the scares began. Since then, the great American public has lived in fear of attack. Killer bees are where real life meets Hollywood, and mass hysteria sets in. The morning headline on 20th May 1998 broke the news: 'Killer Bees Take First Californian Victim.'

'You mean to say that you went running in them?'

The strap underneath gave the full story: 'Dog's Death is First in Golden State Blamed on Africanised Bees.' The victim was a pit bull called Killer. Orson Welles could have written the copy. On 16th March 1999 another story broke: 'Killer Bees Reach Northern LA County. Hive Discovered in Oak Tree in Spot 13 Miles Northwest of Downtown Los Angeles.' The citadel itself was about to be invaded. They were reported to be moving north at an alarming rate of fifty miles per year.

My daughter was the first to turn our terrifying encounter to her advantage. As soon as we were safely back at the lovely Nosara Lodge, sitting high in the hills above the creek, she took out her crayons and wrote 'Brave List'. She began: 'Things I should have for being brave. Crisps. Sweets. Fanta. Kisses. Cuddles.' Then, as an afterthought, she wrote in very large, very childish writing, 'BEWEAR OF KILLER BEES.' My own list was less extensive. It consisted of just one item: 'Very Many Cold Imperials.' Imperial was the excellent local beer. I added my own motto: 'BEE ALERT.'

We sat drinking on the balcony, telling each other tales. A poster was pinned on the wall above us, 'Serpientes Venenosas de Costa Rica' (Venomous Snakes of Costa Rica), but no warnings about killer bees. As the night wore on and the empty Imperial bottles lined up, we became more and more brave. Eckhard had had to steer the boat with his eyes closed for 15 whole minutes, trying to outchase the swarm. They had followed us for a good 500 metres along the middle of the creek! We were being eaten alive!

Then Eckhard, an honest man, muttered, 'It's always the small animals, not the big ones, that get you. Better five sharks than twenty killer bees.'

Brave Eckhard sloped off back to his *rancho* to lie in his hammock. 'My favourite place,' he said quietly. We sat up late, downing Imperials until the tale of the creek was quite fantastical. Night came in, darkening the broad brown ribbon of the creek, looking so peaceful below us. But we knew that somewhere, in that thick green undergrowth, lurked a swarm of killer bees waiting for their prey.

The irresistible young McEntee

MY CONFESSION

Veteran Fleet Street hack **JOHN McENTEE** *was sexually abused by a man of the cloth from the age of eight – and, he says, it did him absolutely no harm at all*

Brother Timothy first noticed it. Newly arrived at the De La Salle primary school in Ireland's border county of Cavan, he had taken over the junior flageolet band. Putting the band members through their paces, he was astonished to discover one gangly ten-year-old who couldn't play the instrument. That youngster was me, and I couldn't play because I was a favourite of Timothy's predecessor, Brother Francis, who had vanished in a puff of smoke amid a flurry of claims that he had interfered with young pupils at the school. I was one of the prepubescent boys that Brother Francis had 'fiddled' with.

With half of Ireland now discovering they had been abused by priests or brothers or nuns, and the Irish Prime Minister at war with the Vatican over its alleged cover-up, I risk opprobrium by declaring that it did me no harm – no damage, no trauma, no nightmares. And unless the De La Salle order is poised with a massive cheque to compensate me for my trauma, I am willing to confess that my similarly singled-out classmates and I have grown up normally and got on with our lives. We don't yearn for an earnest documentary about our plight. Much as I would love to be interviewed with my face pixellated, blathering about the abuse, I am resigned to the reality: it didn't matter. And he was an excellent teacher to boot.

It started at about the age of eight when the charismatic Brother Francis took charge of us. He took a shine to me along with about half a dozen of my classmates, and I was flattered. The only criterion for selection seems to have

been looks. If you were plug ugly or, as some of the poorer boys were, filthy, you were in no danger of the discreet summons to Francis's knee during class.

A swarthy, dark-haired Errol Flynn lookalike, Francis was equally popular with our mothers. He taught us arithmetic, English, Irish, geography, history and religious instruction. After class he organised the junior football league and ran the school's flageolet band.

Much as I would love to be interviewed with my face pixellated, blathering about the abuse, it didn't matter

For an eight-year-old it was considered quite a privilege to be selected for Francis's sexual attention. Like my friends, I knew it was wrong, but we were not then sexually awake. What he did, and we acquiesced in, was simply naughty, like wetting your trousers.

His technique never varied. A test or essay would be signalled on the blackboard and it was heads down as we scribbled feverishly. 'John,' he would say, beckoning with his finger as he sat behind his desk at the top of the classroom. 'Can you come up here for a word?'

It didn't seem odd being asked to sit on his soutane-shrouded lap. 'Your mother,' he would begin, 'is very keen for you to join the band. Would you like that?'

'Yes, brother,' I would answer as his right hand wandered up my exposed knee towards the hem of my short trousers. 'Well, I can arrange that,' Francis would whisper as his

hand reached my thigh and disappeared under the trews. Reaching my dormant penis he would stroke and twiddle, all the time droning on about my progress in the class. I was too young to be aroused, but I recall the acute sense of danger and illicitness. I can't remember if Francis was aroused beneath the folds of his black soutane. The 'chat' might last fifteen minutes before I was told to return to my seat.

My friends Barry and Brendan had similar experiences: after class we would congregate in the cloakroom to discuss and giggle about what happened.

There was an unspoken rule that we didn't tell our parents. Like the other recipients of Francis's favours, I did extremely well academically. But my lack of skill on the football field was there for all to see. My mother considered Francis almost a saint for his efforts to turn me into a footballer. When she saw the band perform she had no idea her son was merely running his fingers over a silent flageolet.

Perversely, the boys who were not sexually fiddled with were subject to regular beatings. One was ordered to drop his trousers in front of the entire class while Brother Francis whacked

'Get me something to apologise for, Miss Jones'

him on the bottom with a thin cane. His weeping face stared at us, and we stared mutely back, watching the brutality in a manner reminiscent of William Golding's feral schoolboys in *Lord of the Flies*.

Older pupils along the corridor received even more harsh physical punishment from Brother Cyril. Long after Brother Francis's abrupt departure, we were to learn Irish the hard way under the brutality of Brother Cyril. A demented Gaelic nationalist, he would stand before a terrified twelve-year-old, demand he would answer in Irish, and when the petrified youngster faltered in his delivery, Cyril would unleash a barrage of open-handed slaps on both ears. He was known to punch and to draw blood with his cane.

In my final year Cyril taught me Irish through ritual thumpings. During one winter class he failed to notice the edge of his tatty soutane catching on the wire surround of the glowing, portable oil heater. We watched in fascination as the cloth began to smoulder, and hoped for Cyril's total immolation. But then one boy raised his hand and declared in pidgin Gaelic, 'Briar, briar ta do soutane ag tine' ('Brother, brother your soutane is on fire'). Needless to say, we tortured Cyril's rescuer in the playground afterwards.

But back to Brother Francis. Eventually I decided to tell my mother about his regular fumblings. She simply didn't believe me: she thought it was a foul slur on an excellent teacher and devout brother. But the game was up for Francis. Other mothers were being alerted by my chums, and one took her little darling's claims seriously enough to complain to the head brother.

We returned from the Easter holidays to discover that we were now in Brother Timothy's class. We were genuinely upset at Brother Francis's departure. He had been transferred to the De La Salle operation in South Africa.

Brother Timothy took over the running of the band, changing the instrument from flageolet to recorder. As a regular band member I was auditioned by the new boss. 'But you can't play!' he exclaimed, consulting his file. 'And you've been in the band for nearly a year.'

Needless to say, I never told Brother Timothy why I was in the band in the first place.

EXPAT
JOHN HUMPHREYS

Areopoli, Greece

JUST DOWN the coast from the village where I live is a town which used to be called Tsimova. It's now called Areopoli because of what happened there one March day in 1821: the local Greek chieftain, Mavromikhalis, began an uprising against the overlordship of the Turks; ten years of hard fighting later much of modern-day Greece was free from Turkish rule. To honour its role, the town was renamed Areopoli – after Ares, Greek god of war – and every year holds a ceremony of thanksgiving. I usually attend. That's how I met Colin.

Among the soberly dressed Greek crowd he was hard to miss in his pink T-shirt, cut-off denims and lime-green Crocs. Seeing him, I experienced my usual ambivalence on encountering tourists. On the one hand, here was a chance to impress a newcomer with my local knowledge. On the other, I liked to mix in with the Greeks, and striking up a conversation with every visiting foreigner didn't help – especially when the foreigner looked as foreign as this one did.

In the event, I was spared the decision. He wandered over to me and said, 'What's going on here, mate?' Slightly miffed at being so readily spotted as a foreigner myself, I told him – the Greeks were celebrating their revolt against the Turks, which started in this town. Colin looked thoughtful for a moment, then his face lit up – 'Like in that film, *Five Hundred*, right? It was the Spartans fighting the Turks? That was here, then, was it?', and he laughed a peculiarly loud and penetrating laugh, causing several heads to turn.

Colin's history was adrift by about 2,500 years and a couple of hundred miles, and shaky in several other respects as well. It was *three* hundred Spartans under their king, Leonidas, who had held the pass at Thermopylae in 480 BC, and it was the Persians, not the Turks, who had been the invaders. I was about to set him straight when the

military band, which had been standing at ease, smoking furtively, suddenly struck up a stirring patriotic air. Up the cobbled streets from the town centre appeared the parade – men dressed in fustanelas, firing flint-lock pistols skywards, priests in their dark robes swinging censers, solid-looking representatives of the local municipality, and school children in period costume.

The parade halted in front of the statue of Mavromikhalis for patriotic speeches and the laying of wreaths. Colin snapped away with his digital camera and periodically unleashed his formidable laugh. He had just opened his mouth to ask me a question when three of the Hellenic Air Force's ageing jets screamed low overhead. As their sound died away the band struck up again. Colin was still trying to say something; I led him towards the back of the crowd and into a small café.

The only other customers were three pairs of elderly men playing backgammon. We took a table and Colin showed me the shots on his camera – he was a pretty good photographer. I began to feel obscurely guilty about my snobbish self-consciousness at being seen with him. Then the waitress came over and asked me, in Greek, what I wanted. I ordered an ouzo, which she brought before taking Colin's order. He asked whether he could try it, sipped it gingerly, and then said 'Bloody hell!' a bit too loudly for my comfort. Six craggy Greek faces turned to study us impassively. 'And what would you like to drink?' the waitress asked him in English. 'Coffee,' he said. 'What kind?' she asked. He gazed around to where the old Greeks sat staring at us, thimble-sized cups of dark brew clutched in their hands, then turned back to her. 'Turkish,' he said, beaming.

I winced. For a moment it was like being trapped inside an H M Bateman cartoon – I waited for jaws to drop open, eyebrows to fly up and hats to take flight in a storm of outrage. But the Greeks just chuckled and shook their heads and nudged each other, and the waitress smiled and said to Colin, 'We call it "Greek".' Then she turned to me, switched back to her own language, and said, 'Especially today!' Outside in the square the statue of the Turk-slaughtering Mavromikhalis stood gesturing fiercely in the spring sunshine amidst the fluttering of white and blue flags, and the band was standing at ease, lighting up once again.

KEEP DANCING!

Veteran writer and illustrator
SHIRLEY HUGHES has
accompanied her reminiscences
for The Oldie with illustrations
and covers. We look back at
a selection of her work

Main picture: cover illustration from February 2011, in which Shirley wrote a piece remembering ballroom dancing in 1941. The illustrations of shy boys and waiting girls and a couple dancing (*above and facing page*) accompanied the feature.

Right, middle: a piece from September 2013 recalled her time studying dress design and fashion drawing at the Liverpool School of Art in the late Forties, an important grounding for future life as an illustrator. *Below*: one of Shirley's fashion illustrations from that time.

Below, middle: Self-portrait as a child, drawing still-life watercolours.

Right and below, right: Going to the cinema during the war was an important and exciting pastime, complete with fleas and boiled sweets... From January 2012

Evening Gown —

Detour round *my father*

Artist, adulterer, foreign correspondent, pilot – Dick Wyndham made a great bohemian but a lousy father, says **JOAN WYNDHAM**

Dick Wyndham, my father, was brought up at Clouds in Dorset, one of the great Victorian country houses of the day. The walls were hung with Pre-Raphaelites, the floors carpeted by William Morris. His family loved to entertain the 'Souls', a group of poets, painters and politicians devoted to the Arts and their own egos. The whole house vibrated with good talk, intellectual games and music from the Great Hall, where Isadora Duncan loved to dance. But my father was just a normal, grubby little boy, known to his family as Dirty Dick.

In 1914, when war broke out, he became the scruffiest soldier in the Royal Rifle Corps. His buttons were always undone, and the art of puttee-winding totally foxed him. Sometimes he would appear on parade in his bedroom slippers. Nevertheless, he made a good officer and was awarded the MC.

He later developed a passion for sketching and spent a few weeks on his own in Venice, drawing the old *palazzi*. One day he was introduced to the Vorticist painter Wyndham Lewis. At the word 'Clouds', Lewis's ears pricked up. Soon Dick was Lewis's patron, paying him monthly sums of money in return for lessons. If the money was ever late, he'd get a rude letter: 'Where's my fucking stipend?' But when Dick lost his money in the Wall Street Crash, Lewis became a vicious enemy. Poking fun at what he called 'Champagne Bohemians' in his book *The Apes of God*, Lewis caricatured Dick as 'the Authentic Ape, the World's Prize Ape'. He went on to describe Dick in gruesome detail: conceited, foolish, a clumsy mover and a great farter, he lived in a glass vacuum in which his own image was reflected from every wall.

He was posted as ADC to Field Marshal Sir John French. French had with him his mistress (my grandmother, Wendy Bennett), to whom he used to write 'Darling Wendy', signed 'Peter Pan'. Wendy's daughter, Iris, was with her – my beautiful, innocent mother, with her flat chest, long feet and striking violet eyes.

Dick fell for her instantly, and asked her to marry him. They were both virgins, with nothing between them but a chaste kiss behind the conservatory. The day before the wedding, Iris asked her mother for a few tips. Surely this once-famous beauty and *grande horizontale* must know a thing or two. 'Tell me, Mummy, what should I do to please a man?' 'Always wear lots of scent, and never let him see you clean your teeth.' Armed with these counsels, she married, resplendent in satin and pearls, and later suffered a horrendous first night. They practically tore each other to pieces, and had to go to a doctor the next day to find out how 'it' was done.

Their first months at Clouds were pleasant enough. But Dick longed for a son and heir, and when I popped out he seemed to lose all interest in his marriage. Admittedly I was not a particularly delightful child, judging from my mother's entry in her 'Baby's Progress' book: 'Joan bites her nails, dribbles incessantly, is clumsy, obstinate and contrary.' No wonder that he soon fled to London to console himself with the company of more mature women. The last straw came when Iris caught him kissing the Marquess of Queensbury behind the Christmas tree. She divorced him, and moved with me to London, where she soon acquired a female companion who converted her to Catholicism.

My poor mother, now forbidden to re-marry, consoled herself in bed with a bar of Bournville, a glass of milk and a detective novel. One night, after a few sherries, she told me that my father was now a famous painter.

Two years later I was staying with my grandfather in the country when a big open-topped Rolls roared up to the gates and out came a tall, gangling figure who stared at me in puzzlement. Suddenly he realised that I was his daughter, and

FATTYPUFFS — K.J.Lamb

REMEMBER WE'RE ON A DIET...

...SO NO SNACKING BETWEEN SNACKS!

we hugged and kissed. I had to call him 'Daddy Dick', not Daddy, as this sounded more exciting and less odiously parental. In the evening there were charades, for Dick loved dressing up.

As I got older, Dick began to take a vague sort of interest in me, and invited me one night to a party given by his friend Cyril Connolly. It was full of clever, bitchy people – like being thrown into a bowl of piranhas. Dick vanished and I was terrified, but luckily Arthur Koestler befriended me. Watching Dick stumbling off myopically, in search of fresh talent, he laughed unkindly. 'We have a saying: you can always tell when a pretty girl comes into the room because Dick takes his glasses off.'

As we left, Dick said in a voice of bewilderment, 'Do you know, some of my friends seem to think you are rather prettah.' This cheered me up no end.

In return, I took him on a pub crawl of all the sleaziest hangouts: the Fitzroy, the Burglar's Rest and the Wheatsheaf. We met lots of louche characters, all wanting either to pinch my bottom or borrow money. Dick was horrified, 'Is this your set, Joanie?'

In the taxi on the way home something awful happened. Dick, who was now drunk, forgot who I was, and made his usual mental connection – taxi, girl, make pass. He began to kiss me passionately and tried to undo my shirt. Thank God we were nearly home. Afterwards I don't think he remembered anything about it.

Soon after this he got rid of Clouds, that albatross around his neck, and moved into Tickerage Mill, a much smaller and cosier house where he entertained such celebrities as Cyril Connolly, Stephen Spender, Tom Driberg and Constant Lambert, plus any girls he fancied. His cellar was famous, and so were his house parties – bathing,

> *Out of a big open-topped Rolls stepped a tall gangling figure who stared at me in puzzlement. Suddenly he realised I was his daughter*

fireworks, fancy dress and croquet on the lawn at night by the light of cigars. Dinner was an elaborate affair, with at least six magnums of the finest claret. Connolly was Dick's greatest friend, and also his sternest critic. 'Dick's nails were always black,' he wrote, 'his fly-buttons undone, his teeth yellow and his chin unshaven. Nevertheless it was impossible to resist the charm and humour of this middle-aged schoolboy, this battered Bulldog Drummond, this Don Giovanni in rags.'

Dick Wyndham and Joan

Dick got a job as Foreign Correspondent in the Middle East for the *Sunday Times*, where he used his little Moth plane to hop from scoop to scoop.

In London he was based at the Hyde Park Hotel. There he worked on his 'swindle sheets', his enormous bogus expenses. He always carried a shabby leather bag containing Valium, whisky,

cigarettes and a battered black book containing short, cryptic notes – 'red tie, toothbrush moustache, *very* influential' or 'small breasts, tight bottom, free on Wednesdays'.

Some months later, back in the Middle East, he crashed in the mountains of Iran and walked for miles with frostbitten feet, living on sunflower seeds. I was in the maternity ward, having just given birth to my second child, when a strange tall man lurched in on crutches. He was wearing a long, dirty sheepskin coat, and bandages on his feet. 'Looking for my daughtah!' he said, gazing myopically around. He had obviously forgotten my name, but finally recognised me.

Proudly, I showed him my baby. 'Hideous, isn't it? They all are!' I was delighted he had managed to come, and hoped for a real family relationship in the future, but that was the last time I was to see him.

One day in May I was reading the *Times* at breakfast when my heart stopped beating. 'Dick Wyndham died today on the northern outskirts of Jerusalem. Wearing Arab Legion uniform, he stood up to photograph the fighting between the Arabs and the Israelis. He was hit by a sniper's bullet, and died instantly.'

Ian Fleming's obituary followed. 'One of the great Bohemians of his age, moving arrogantly through the circles of his time with one foot in White's and the other in Bloomsbury – we saw in his insolent but gentle brilliance those qualities of "panache" and chivalry which are the inheritance of great Englishmen.'

A few days later, I was summoned to lunch by Cyril Connolly. There was a box of papers to be gone through, 'but first, of course, we should go down to Tickerage and hide the whips.' Cyril saw my puzzled look. 'Good God, girl, didn't you know your father was one of England's most famous flagellists? Some of the women who came to Tickerage spent a lot of their time up trees!'

After a grand and moving memorial service, I made for the nearest pub, where I ordered a large whisky and drank a farewell toast to the father I tried so hard to love, but never really knew.

CYPRESSUS ACCURSIDII

*As an environment minister under Labour, **CHRIS MULLIN** had modest aims, one of which was to rein in the dreaded leylandii that was spreading across our suburbs*

Illustrated by Martin Honeysett

'You aren't going to be here long. Don't try to change the world. Just pick two or three issues where you may be able to make a difference and leave the rest.' Such was the sensible advice offered to me by the Permanent Secretary, Sir Richard Mottram, on the first day of my eighteen undistinguished months as a junior minister in the Environment department.

I chose three modest aims: regulating the growth of leylandii trees, placing limits on night flights over London and making discretionary the payment of housing benefit to slum landlords. On the face of it these were all goals that ought to have been easily achievable, but in practice each proved a struggle.

Leylandii are a cause of warfare in the suburbs. The problem is that they are forest trees wholly unsuited to suburban gardens. They grow at the rate of three or four feet a year, up to a height of a hundred feet and, unless maintained (which many aren't), they swiftly cast a dark shadow over a neighbour's garden. Sometimes the damage is inadvertent. Sometimes leylandii are used as a weapon.

People whose lives were blighted by the remorseless growth of leylandii spent fortunes on legal actions. To no avail. Local authorities were powerless. The Environment department received hundreds of letters each year, asking for the law to be changed. It ought to have been simple enough. All that was needed was a minor amendment to the planning law, giving a local authority the power to require hedges to be maintained at a reasonable height.

Various private members' Bills had attempted to resolve the matter, but all came to grief. By the time I came on the scene it was clear that legislation was the only solution. 'If we can't sort out something as simple as this,' I said to myself, 'we might as well all go home.' Inevitably, however, it proved a great deal more complicated than I could ever have imagined.

Objections flowed in from every quarter: the Home Office, the Lord Chancellor, Downing Street... It was said that the Prime Minister

Leylandii are a cause of warfare in the suburbs, and sometimes used as a weapon

himself had personally vetoed legislation. It was suggested that he was likely to veto even a consultation that might lead to legislation. 'What's the problem?' I asked the man who came from Number 10 bearing the bad tidings. 'I bet the Prime Minister hasn't devoted more than thirty seconds of his time to this.' He confirmed that this was so. I pressed him and reluctantly he disgorged two names. Jonathan Powell and Anji Hunter, respectively the Prime Minister's chief of staff and personal assistant.

'Anji Hunter? Where does she fit in?' 'The Prime Minister values her political antennae.'

I later heard that she had seen Rory Bremner making jokes about the 'nanny state' (a favourite *Daily Mail* theme, although on this issue even the *Mail* was onside). Apparently, this contained the line, 'Do you know, the government is even proposing to regulate the size of hedges?' Result: our entire effort kiboshed.

We conducted yet another consultation. Needless to say, it reached the same conclusion: namely, that only a change in the law would make any difference. Again, needless to say, we were instructed to ignore the conclusion and opt instead for a 'code of conduct', always the last resort of governments reluctant to confront a vested interest.

In co-operation with the garden centre industry (which was the cause of the problem), a leaflet was produced. A meeting to consider a draft with officials was held in the office of the Environment Minister, Michael Meacher. It was a scene from *Yes Minister*. 'Where,' asked Michael, 'does it actually say that it is not a good idea to plant leylandii?'

'Ah, well, Minister, it doesn't quite put it as boldly as that. We have to be careful not to upset the industry.'

In fact, as one of the officials cheerfully pointed out, the leaflet was drafted in a way that could actually be seen as encouraging the growing of leylandii – the exact opposite of what we were trying to achieve.

Several more years elapsed, and much energy wasted on displacement activity, before the government was finally persuaded to legislate. By this time I was long gone, though I continued to pursue the matter from the backbenches. Eventually, a clause was introduced into the Anti-social Behaviour Act giving local authorities the power to regulate hedges more than two metres in height. It came into force from June 2005.

Inevitably, it contained a loophole. An order to cut back a hedge cannot be issued if there is a danger that by doing so it is likely to kill the trees (who was the far-sighted idiot who inserted that?) which in many cases, it would. Some local authorities immediately attempted to sabotage the new law by charging outrageous fees for taking up complaints. Others, in fairness, charged nothing.

Has it worked? Hard to tell. To be sure, the number of complaints has gone down, which suggests that something has changed for the better. A quick surf of the internet, however, reveals that garden centres are still marketing the accursed leylandii as aggressively as ever. Some things never change.

Alive on the ocean wave

Lifeboats, helicopter airlifts, even jaywalking: **WILFRED DE'ATH** *is looking for the ride of his life*

I HAVE MADE more than 300 crossings with Brittany Ferries over the years; my main complaint being that nothing ever happens. Until the other day, that is, when four hours out of St Malo we looked out of the portholes to see the lifeboats being lowered. The stupid captain announced (in French) that this was merely an emergency drill, but mild panic set in among the English passengers who, of course, hadn't understood. Yours truly, who can never resist a bit of mischief, added fuel to the flames by yelling 'Women and children first' at the top of his voice...

What had begun as a simple practice soon turned into a genuine crisis. The first thing that happened was that one of the emergency chutes became disconnected from the mother ship and floated off into the Channel. Then a frightened old man had a heart attack, brought on, no doubt, by all the excitement. They had to radio for a French naval helicopter from Cherbourg to airlift the poor old boy to hospital. The pilot did a grand job, dropping the copter onto a bit of deck about the size of my dining-room table. I was beside myself with excitement.

We got into Portsmouth two hours late as a result of all this, but I felt more 'alive' than I had done in years – even though I missed my last train to Cambridge. The terrible fact is that, at the age of 74, I am becoming an adrenaline junkie. There are a few other things that make me feel more 'alive':

Shoplifting. Successful theft, as Truman Capote once remarked, is exhilarating. Nothing compares with the satisfaction of walking out of Tesco with a tin of baked beans under your cap. (A friend of mine, a doctor, regularly puts on a new suit in the changing room at M&S and walks out, leaving his old one behind. He does this about once a month. He has never been caught.)

Hotel bilking. Check out the entrances and exits the night you arrive and walk out next morning before they present you with the bill. If you are like me, you will feel intensely happy as you do so. (I was caught once – in Pau in the Pyrenees – when the owner followed me to the station on his motorbike.)

Jaywalking. I take great pleasure in crossing against the traffic and watching the cars grind to a halt. This is, to adapt Nietzsche, really living dangerously, especially in France where all motorists hate all pedestrians.

Running out of money. I usually go to France with less money than I really need. It makes getting home pretty exciting.

Chassez les femmes. I occasionally vow not to eat until I have successfully 'dated' a girl I fancy. Three times out of five I go hungry, of course, but twice I may enjoy a delicious meal in her company. Existentially, this is the most exciting thing of all.

"I expect you really miss the kids."

'Nurse – prepare the patient's wallet for an extraction'

'Stop it, George, that death rattle is so annoying'

The Oldie IN ✚
HOSPITAL

'When my old TV got like this I just gave it a whack'

HE CAN'T REMEMBER WHO HE IS

LET'S TELL HIM HE'S NICK CLEGG

A night at the OPERA

Beleaguered understudies, forgotten lines, noises off... **STAFFORD DEAN** *tells some tales about opera's less edifying moments*

A member of the management coming through the curtains to make an announcement before the overture usually means only one thing – the indisposition of a member of the cast. Yet once they have accepted the disappointment of their favourite singer being unable to appear, British audiences are well known for their generous support of the understudy.

However, Dame Lilian Baylis, the administrator of Sadler's Wells Opera, could be rather less than generous on such occasions. She was once obliged to put on a young understudy who had, shall we say, rather less than *un succès fou*, and, as the young lady was sitting in her dressing-room after the performance surrounded by family and friends trying to persuade her that she had done very well, the head of Dame Lilian appeared round the door. Conversation ceased as they waited for some form of encouragement, but there was to be none. 'Had your chance. Missed it!' she said firmly, and disappeared.

Things at Aldeburgh were hardly better when the young Robert Tear was understudying Peter Pears. It had been decided that he should take Peter's place for one performance as the Madwoman in *Curlew River*, which Benjamin Britten and Peter would attend. They were both known to come round after the show to give extensive critiques and Bob waited in his dressing room, reasonably confident of his contribution. Eventually, he heard Ben leaving the dressing-room next door and braced himself for the composer's verdict. The footsteps, however, continued straight

Lilian Baylis: not one to mince words

past his door. A minute or two later, Peter Pears looked in. 'Lipstick terribly pale,' he said.

When Sadler's Wells mounted a new production of *Carmen*, the bass who had sung Zuniga in the previous production was asked to be on standby. Unfortunately for him, a new translation had been commissioned, and when he was phoned a few days after the opening to be told that he would have to go on that night, he found himself rather less *au fait* with the dialogue than he might have wished. It was the tradition at the Wells to do without a prompt-box and, if help was required, the stage manager provided assistance from stage right. The understudy began confidently but, as his scene with Carmen progressed, one was aware that he was relying more and more on the whispered prompts. Eventually, all pretence was shattered when he turned from Carmen to the stage manager and, in a broad New Zealand accent, said, 'I beg yer pardon?'

Dialogue is often a problem for opera singers. I remember a wonderful Australian bass called Stanley Clarkson who came to England quite late in his career, which had been in concert and oratorio. One of his first roles at the Wells was Sarastro in *The Magic Flute*. By the dress rehearsal he was still uneasy with the dialogue at the beginning of the second act. His understudy was a young bass singing the second priest and standing beside him as Stanley struggled to remember his lines. Eventually Stan ground to a halt and turned to the now giggling priest, saying 'And it's not bloody funny, either!'

It was apparent that the soprano had left herself less time to memorise the role than she should have...

Fortunately, it was a 'closed' dress rehearsal, but at Covent Garden such occasions are often open to an invited audience. A number of years ago a favourite international soprano was returning to sing Rosalinde in *Die Fledermaus* and it was soon apparent in rehearsals that she had left herself less time to memorise the role than she should have. When the day of the public dress rehearsal arrived, to be sure that she received the support she needed she sent for the prompter and told him to remember to speak up. And speak up he did! My manager, who was present, reported that 'every line was a duet, every duet was a trio and when she said "Hush, I hear voices", the audience collapsed!'

PHOTO COURTESY OF: GETTY IMAGES

CARDUS
THE LAST ADVENTURE

In 1973 a young journalist on a regional paper sent a fan letter to the distinguished cricket and music writer Sir Neville Cardus, igniting an intense friendship which lasted until Cardus's death.
ELIZABETH GRICE *looks back*

When I first spluttered up to Bickenhall Mansions from the country in a mustard-coloured Mini, Sir Neville Cardus was already waiting on the steps, wearing a light grey suit, brown suede shoes and an air of mild agitation. He had a cigarette on. His silver hair was brushed back with some kind of unguent and he smelled of Eau Sauvage. 'I somehow fancied I'd be able to identify you at sight,' he said.

I had written him a fan letter after seeing a series of television programmes about his early days in Manchester and his illustrious career as music critic and cricket writer for the *Manchester Guardian*. Four days later, I was being propelled fiercely by the elbow across three lanes of traffic to the restaurant in Baker Street where he dined every night. Cardus, well into his eighties, looked as loose and thin as a puppet and walked with little high-stepping movements as though the road was made of burning coals, but he had a grip of iron.

To this same table at the London Steak House, week after week for years, Cardus had invited singers, actresses, instrumentalists, music critics, sports commentators – and young journalists. I was in the latter category, with the evident advantage of being female. Daniel Barenboim ('young Danny') was a regular. The actress Wendy Hiller was advising him on what he called 'acqua-punta' (acupuncture) for his aches. Nicholas de Jongh of the *Guardian* gave him newspaper gossip. Else Mayer-Lismann talked to him about her opera school. The Garrick Club was where he took another layer of friends: conductors, editors and actors.

Cardus called me 'my young journalist friend from Ipswich', pronouncing 'Ipswich' with Bracknellian disdain. It summed up for him the outer reaches of provincialism and over the coming months he did his utmost to lever me out of it.

There were three main topics of conversation that evening. Kathleen Ferrier, the contralto he had loved and championed so warmly; the stony-heartedness of the *Guardian* (for not paying him enough and cutting his copy); and the painful state of his feet. 'I have seen three "specialists",' he said with a theatrical pause. 'Each has a different opinion but all are unanimous on one point – the fee.' He demanded details of my job on the *East Anglian Daily Times*. I was to send cuttings of my reviews and editorials without delay. 'Don't ever think of your public, or of your editor,' he warned, jabbing a bony finger into my arm.

He chopped his Dover sole into a mush and pushed it around his plate. After coffee, he always lit up, ate two Bendicks' mint chocolates, rolled the gold paper into little balls and put them in his pocket. When he

On 'visitation days', as he called them, I would bring Gorgonzola cheese and digestive biscuits and he would supply the claret

flicked out his cheque book to pay, it was covered in big-nosed cartoons of Sir Adrian Boult and Otto Klemperer. Cardus had beautiful handwriting and he loved to draw caricatures.

From the autumn of 1973, I visited his green-upholstered subterranean flat every month for more than a year and we exchanged letters most days. 'I seem to have known you for years,' he said. The rooms smelled of old pipe tobacco. The kitchen was foreign territory. He had an early Lowry over his mantelpiece but almost no money in the bank. On 'visitation days', as he

called them, I would bring Gorgonzola cheese and digestive biscuits and he would supply the claret. He wanted to know what I'd been writing and whom I'd interviewed. There was no need to be impatient, he said, because at my age (26), he was still collecting burial insurance from people who could hardly afford to live, let alone save for a decent Lancashire funeral.

We listened to Kathleen singing *Das Lied von der Erde* or Brahms's *Alto Rhapsody*, followed by other 'consolations of age' – Mozart's Clarinet Concerto, Elgar's Cello Concerto. His response to music that soothed his soul was a low, tuneless moan. Then, if the omnipresent aches in his feet were not too bad, we would walk to Regent's Park to feed the ducks.

Cardus had published enduring books on music and cricket, as well as three exquisite memoirs, but at heart he was as vulnerable as a young reporter hoping to do well.

'He's trying to kick-start the housing market'

'Nothing of mine has been printed in the *Guardian* for four weeks,' he moaned – aged 85. 'Somehow it all depresses me, though really I shouldn't care less. But I am, like any true journalist, always pleased to see myself in the paper, even if distorted.'

He complained that his review of Artur Rubinstein's autobiography, submitted six weeks earlier, still had not appeared. 'They prefer Greenfield [Edward Greenfield, his successor as music critic] writing about The Beatles. I am amused rather than annoyed.' He didn't sound amused, though.

After a few months, impatient that I had not landed a job in London, he had an idea. Against his better judgement and the message from his feet, this man who had travelled not much further than Lord's cricket ground for the last three years, and had stopped going to concerts, would come to 'sub-provincial' Ipswich.

I booked him into the Great White Horse Hotel, featured in *The Pickwick Papers*. He liked the thought that Dickens's shade might come to him during a sleepless night. Frankly, it was an anxious couple of days because he did not really seem up to the expedition, physically, but he claimed it had been 'an experience of rare wonder'. Did he mean that his unscheduled visit to the sports department of the *East Anglian Daily Times* had a pleasing touch of celebrity about it? Or that the paper's music critic, Diapason, treated him like a god? Or was he just chuffed to have done something so utterly improbable? 'My Ipswich pilgrimage,' he called it. I can still see him in my mother's garden, dressed in the best of his three identical

double-breasted suits, demonstrating his slow off-breaks with an apple.

He struck up a friendship with Harold Evans, editor of the *Sunday Times*, who had published a long reflection by him about listening to music in old age. He badgered Evans to see me and in October 1974 his kindly intervention paid off: I joined the paper.

Later that year, we travelled to Manchester, where the BBC made two programmes of Neville Cardus and John Arlott in conversation. 'Bring a needle and some grey cotton,' he said. 'I am certain that buttons are about to fall from my grey suit like autumn leaves.' When the recording was over, the two men argued far into the night about the finest novel in the English language. Arlott nominated *Tess of the D'Urbervilles*. Cardus said it was *Zuleika Dobson*. He liked the humour. 'So witty, so cleansing in this muddy world.'

His next adventure was to have been Vienna. 'We must walk together in the Wienerwald,' he said, possibly hoping to reprise old romances. In anticipation, he called his tailor. The tailor was to take away, and revive, some old suits and overcoats and to make a new one. 'He took measurements for a new suit (which he said I need not pay for just yet) and said: "You have lost pounds." In fact, I can scarcely find myself in bed when I wake in the dead of night.'

Neville died a few months later, in February 1975, still making plans and schemes; still poking fun at old age. When we sorted his clothes, the pockets of the new grey suit, and several of the old ones, were lined with small balls of gold foil.

To B&B or not to B&B?

That was the question for **ZENGA LONGMORE** as she entered the ranks of the homeless

Illustration by Martin Honeysett

When my eight-year-old daughter Omalara discovered she was moving into a hotel, she leapt three feet in the air like a gaffed salmon. Her reflex reaction was to pick up the phone to deliver the good news to her best friend Stacey. 'Yep! It's gonna be a real hotel! It'll have all the stuff that hotels have! I'll never have to make my own bed again!'

How could I have the heart to tell her that the hotel we were about to move into was in fact a hostel for the homeless? Far from chambermaids and room service, I envisaged cockroach-infested kitchens and evil-smelling communal bathrooms.

After living happily in rented accommodation for eight years, a new and evil landlord had decided to cast us out into the snow, sell the flat and make a quick and easy profit. We had too much furniture to consider renting again. The only solution was to throw ourselves onto the mercy of our local council. Sadly for us, Shylock could have given our local council a lesson or two in mercy.

To step into the homeless section of the housing office was to enter into the last refuge of the damned. Dismal Somali families with at least four crying babies apiece sat silent and glum amidst bursting bin liners filled with all their worldly possessions. Bosnians, West Africans and the odd Irish family sat or stood in a state of similar dejection. Housing officers could be heard shouting at the hopeful supplicants. 'All the B&Bs are full. Understand? Full! You will have to come back tomorrow.'

Infants howled and screamed. Here are the people, I thought, about whom you read in the *Daily Mail*: refugees who supposedly live in unequalled splendour at the expense of the rest of us. When it was my turn to be seen, I was met with a sweeping expression of disgust by a granite-faced housing officer. 'You'll be put into a B&B [a euphemism for a homeless hostel – breakfast is certainly not included] for a few months, then you'll move into temporary accommodation.'

'Where will the B&B be?' I asked with tongue-twisting dexterity. 'My daughter goes to a local school. Will it be near?'

'You think you can choose where you want to live! Ha! I'm terribly sorry to inform you,' she said with a bright-eyed smirk, 'that it could be anywhere. We're even moving people as far out as Kent! You'll know where it is on the day that you move. Come here next Wednesday at two o'clock and you'll find out then.'

By the time Wednesday rolled around, all my furniture had been stored by the council, leaving me with two suitcases I was barely able to drag into the council office. Omalara remained as cheerful as ever, keeping up a continual chatter as we joined the damned souls once again and waited to hear where we were about to live.

'You're in Wembley,' Mrs Granite-Face informed us ruefully. Wembley is an easy bus ride from Omalara's school. 'Here's the address. You've got to be there at three o'clock.'

Half an hour later we arrived in a dazzling street of Edwardian villas. Our hostel was a large white house graced with the word 'Hotel' over the door. Only the unkempt garden and overflowing wheelie bins marked it out as a poor relation of the neighbouring dwellings.

We knocked on the door and waited. Nothing happened. A woman appeared in the upstairs window and watched us with terrified eyes, but she did not think to let us in. Over the next two hours, I began to wonder if we were expected to camp in the garden. Just as we were about to turn tail, a suave Italian man pulled up in a zippy red sports car, hopped out and poured out a stream of apologies. He hoped we had not been waiting far too long. Come in, come in! His name was Guido; he was the manager of the hotel. Managers of council-run establishments receive over £200 a week per homeless person. If this hostel housed over thirty occupants, it would explain the car and the self-satisfied smile.

The inside of the building was dismal, sporting peeling wallpaper and split black vinyl chairs. I could almost hear the clonk as Omalara's heart sank.

'Sit down for a while, ladies, while I get your room ready. At the moment I have a very wicked woman staying in your room, but today I throw her out. She have men in the room, she play music, and sometimes she doesn't even turn up at all! Just wait. I get her stuff out of the room.'

So staying, he cantered up the stairs and proceeded to throw plastic bags over the banisters. The occasional tinkle of something valuable breaking could be heard as the bags hit the ground. Omalara and I sat in silence. Suddenly the front door burst open, and in flew a minute black woman, not much taller than Omalara. A tearful two-year-old trailed behind her. The sight of all her worldly goods being thrown down the stairs appeared

to cause her feelings of discomfort. Shaking her tiny frame, she roared like a wounded rhinoceros.

'That's my blasted stuff! What you flippin' doin' with my *rhaaatid* tings, man?'

'So! It's you! I throw you out. You cause too much trouble!'

'Take your bloodclot 'ands off me boombaclot tings!' Thud! Down came a pushchair. 'I'll gut you like a dyaaam fish!' screeched the woman as she gently placed her baby in my arms. So doing, she sprinted up the stairs to proceed with the gutting process. Bangs, crashes and screams were heard from above. 'Is this a nightmare?' whispered Omalara softly.

Shaking her tiny frame, she roared like a wounded rhinoceros. 'That's my blasted stuff! What you flippin' doin' with my rhaaatid tings, man?'

Before I had time to reply, Guido arrived, looking somewhat the worse for wear. 'So sorry, ladies. I'm afraid things are a little difficult at the moment. Why don't you come back tomorrow when everything's a little more sorted out? Oh, and don't forget to sign the visitors' book.'

We staggered away in search of a friend's floor, and slept the sleep of the just. Next day, we returned to find no trace of the previous occupant. Our room was large and quite enchanting, looking on to a flowery garden. Omalara swiftly formed passionate friendships with the children of the occupants, and after two days our room doubled as a local playgroup.

I was not quite so happy with the arrangements, which were very similar to those of an open prison. One was obliged to sign in a mighty book at every coming and going.

Kitchen utensils were instantly stolen if they were not locked away. Guests were not allowed. Guido had a horrible habit of throwing our door open unannounced to check that we were keeping our room tidy enough 'to comply with council rules'. Every so often notes would magically appear on our bed. 'Your daughter's toys MUST be arranged with more neatness.' 'The communal cupboards in the kitchen are FILTHY. Clean them at once.' 'Your room's been too messy for too long. TIDY IT UP.' Unearthly screams could be heard at night. The Ibo family in the room next to ours appeared to cope

with their stress by chanting ceaseless Hail Marys in thundering tones at three o'clock in the morning. The effect was very creepy.

Not less than a month after I moved in, the magic letter arrived informing me that we could move into 'temporary accommodation'. The day I told Guido we were leaving, he smiled knowingly. That afternoon, when I returned with Omalara from school, our door flapped open revealing a room devoid of our television, stereo and video. Guido was the only person with the keys. I suppose he regarded the tenants' electrical equipment as a sort of fringe benefit for all the hard nagging he was required to do.

Ah! It was good to have our own place at last. Only those who have lived in a homeless hostel can possibly know the true pleasures of living, unhindered, in a frightful mess.

THE REBEL — BY BIRCH

'Your dad's so friendly with the local kids—what's his secret?'

'They were locked up together during the Summer riots.'

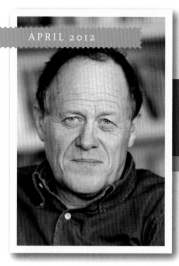

Profitable Wonders
by James Le Fanu

All of a piece

Human fascination with the owl stretches as far back as it is possible to go – they were beautifully portrayed by Palaeolithic artists on the wall of the Chauvet cave in Southern France thirty thousand years ago. The image incised in the yellow ochre rock with a sharpened stick is instantly recognisable, with its large rounded head from which protrude two upright ear tufts. Its plumage is evoked – with an economy worthy of that great owl fancier Picasso – by a dozen tapering vertical lines.

That fascination derives most obviously from the inescapable sense of a supernatural affinity with ourselves – for good or ill. For the Athenians, the owl's physical appearance (particularly those forward-looking eyes), its contemplativeness and its stillness, symbolised the wisdom of their protective goddess Athena. Yet for many societies it is a portent of evil and death – not surprisingly, perhaps, being a creature of the night whose eerie cries the Scottish-American ornithologist Alexander Wilson compared to the 'half-suppressed scream of a person being throttled'. This is also a recurring Shakespearean theme: for Lady Macbeth, the shrieking owl becomes the 'fatal bellman which gives the stern'st goodnight', while for Puck it 'puts the wretch that lies in woe in remembrance of a shroud'.

These contrasting interpretations of the significance of the owl in human affairs are of course related: its seemingly human appearance and attributes being inextricably linked to the challenges of its way of life as a nocturnal predator – so much more so than for those birds of prey that hunt by day.

Silence is essential lest, hovering low over the hedgerows, it alerts its prey. This is made possible by its uniquely designed feathers, described by naturalist Desmond Morris as 'being delicately fringed with serrated edges and a soft velvety surface that dampens the swishing sound of its wings'.

And then there are those disproportionately large forward-

The owl's concave ruff of feathers at the entrance to the ear acts like a satellite receiving dish

facing eyes, so like our own. Not being placed, as in most birds, on either side of its head, they confer the inestimable benefit at dusk of the most acute stereoscopic vision of any avian species. The presence of such large eyes in a relatively small skull would leave insufficient space for the brain were it not for their distinctive structure (fixed and tubular rather than circular and mobile). Unable to turn its eyes, the owl must rotate its head instead, which it is able to do up to an astonishing 270 degrees. This in turn is facilitated by an additional seven vertebrae in its neck (twice the usual number) permitting it to look almost backwards over its shoulder –

'It comes with a set of miniature anti-badger-cull activists and a set of anti-wind-turbine protesters'

as indeed it is portrayed in the Chauvet cave painting.

When its prey, whether fieldmouse or vole, is invisible in the impenetrable darkness of the night, the owl must rely on the exceptional acuity and directionality of its hearing to detect rustling in the undergrowth – the acuity facilitated by a concave ruff of feathers at the entrance to the ear that acts like a satellite receiving dish. As for directionality, owls deploy the technique known as amplitude monopulse (reinvented for human use by radar engineers in World War Two), where the asymmetric positioning of its ears on either side of the head permits it to detect the direction and position of its prey by the minuscule time difference (as little as thirty millionths of a second) it takes for the sound waves to reach either ear. When they coincide precisely the owl is looking directly at its potential victim.

Come the moment of the strike the owl relies not on its beak – short and downward-curved so as not to obscure its field of vision or hearing – but swings forward its four immensely powerful talons to grasp and crush its prey. This in turn is facilitated by two further unique adaptations: a fully mobile front outer toe that can switch to face backwards so as to strengthen the grip, and rough adherent tissue – like Velcro – on the under-surface of its feet.

The impressive aspect of each of these unique adaptations for nocturnal hunting is not just that they confer on the owl what might seem almost unearthly powers, but that they are all 'of a piece' to achieve its intended purpose. In this, the owl exemplifies, to a remarkable degree, the 'laws of correlation' originally proposed by the great nineteenth-century natural historian Georges Cuvier – where every species 'forms a distinctive whole, a unique and perfect system whose parts mutually correspond and concur to the same definitive end.'

![once met...]

Trevor Howard

DUSTY ROADES *remembers a brief encounter with the cricket-loving character actor nearly 55 years ago*

Trevor Howard

It was a bright summer morning in 1956 and our annual Scout fete was to be held that afternoon. It was due to be opened by the captain of our local football team and I telephoned him to confirm that he would be there. His mother answered the telephone and told me that he was not at home – he was holidaying in Spain. Problem: how to find an alternative? Our chairman suggested that we ask Trevor Howard – 'After all, he lives in our village.' This was true, but I did not know him apart from seeing him occasionally at the local public house.

Rather tentatively I went to his house and rang the front door bell. No answer, so I went to the back garden. Trevor Howard was sitting on a deck chair, naked to the waist. The patio doors were open and in the room behind was a television set with a cricket match showing. He looked up, put his whisky down and said, 'What can I do for you, young man?' I told him about the fete and asked if he would be prepared to open it.

'Has somebody let you down?' he asked, and I said 'Yes.' 'Right,' he said, 'where is it and what time?' I told him.

'Right, I will be there, now leave me to the cricket.'

At ten to two there was no sign of our celebrity opener and I began to get worried. But a moment or two later out came Trevor with his wife Helen Cherry. He came to the stage, tapped the microphone, and said how privileged he felt to be asked to open the fete. Along with his wife, he then

He visited every stall, sold autographs and kisses and stayed for well over an hour

visited every stall, talking to the Scouts, saying what a splendid time he was having and spending money on each stall. They sold autographs and kisses, and stayed for well over an hour. As they left I thanked them for spending their time with us.

'Two things,' he said. 'You owe me a double next time we meet in The Gate, and never ask me again.' 'Oh,' I said, 'I thought you enjoyed the afternoon.'

He smiled and replied, 'Young man, I am an actor.'

SEND US YOUR TXT

Got something to say?
Text your comment, followed by your name and where you live to
07563 969088

● Walter, there is nothing embarrassing about braces. It would be embarrassing though if your trousers fell down in a public place, wouldn't it?
Martha, Evesham

● I once lost my trousers in Spain. I was swimming and someone must have stolen them. But I had another pair at the hotel.
Brian, Henley

● My father held that braces were a sign of effeminacy. He always wore a belt.
Sylvia, Hull

● A good belting never did anyone any harm. You can't hit a boy with braces.
Giles, Sutton

● It beats me that people can prattle about braces when the Eurozone is facing collapse.
Terence, Sidcup

● I have never been in favour of the Eurozone. You can't get fish paste in Germany. I blame the Common Market.
Gill, Frinton

● Lighten up, Terence.
Roger, Darlington

● I always take a jar of fish paste with me when I go abroad. There is no law that says you can't.
Penny, Hexham

● I once ruined a perfectly good pair of trousers when I sat on a bench in Denmark which had just been painted. I say good riddance to the Euro.
Neville, Glasgow

● Sheena, you're not the only one to give your wheelie bin a nickname. We call ours the Guardian. Why? Because it's full of rubbish
Marty, Weymouth

A Toast to the
Marmalade Cat

The art of Kathleen Hale, creator of Orlando the Marmalade Cat, has delighted generations of children, and still works its magic on **MERLIN HOLLAND**

We first met forty years ago when I was about eight and she in her mid-fifties. On reflection it was grossly ill-mannered of me to have refused a kiss to one who had already given me so much youthful pleasure, but independence is important at that age and father's old friend or no, I wasn't having any of it. I must have been forgiven, though, for she signed all my well-thumbed Orlando books and sent me a copy of *A Seaside Holiday* a year later 'with love from Orlando, Grace, Pansy, Blanche and Tinkle'.

Thirty years went by, I had a young family of my own and the world seemed to have been taken over, triffid-like, by Mr Men. I turned in despair to the books of my childhood, Orlando amongst others, but I was quite unready for the electric effect which the centre-page spread of *Orlando Buys a Farm* would have on dormant memories. My own reaction aside, their introduction to a new generation was a triumph. 'The pictures are so big I can climb into them,' said my son, faced with pages half his own height. 'That,' explained Kathleen Hale, 'is exactly what I had intended.'

Bringing up her own family in 1934, she was equally frustrated by the lack of imaginative children's books and took to inventing stories to keep them amused. Some time later she complained of the problem to an old friend and editor of the *Cambridge Magazine*, C K Ogden. He offered to translate her tales and include them in a series of pocket books he was publishing for children in Japan if she would write them down with illustrations in black and white. For Kathleen, who had been earning a living as an artist since 1918, the constraints of size and lack of colour were impossible conditions. She knew how children loved large books from watching two or three of them lie on the floor and share *Babar the Elephant*, so she wrote *Orlando's Camping Holiday* and *Orlando's Trip Abroad*, illustrated in seven colours and designed as folio-sized volumes.

For two years her agent tried in vain to place them. Finally *Country Life* agreed to publish but insisted that the printers' in-house lithographer redraw the illustrations so that they could be reproduced as a combination of the four standard printing colours – red, yellow, blue and black. It was a procedure similar to the professional engravers of the 18th and 19th centuries reducing portraits to printable size – competent reproduction, but somehow lacking the spontaneity of the original. It also answers the nagging question of why I never quite loved the cats in *A Camping Holiday* as much as I did in all the later books – they weren't yet entirely Kathleen Hale.

From then on she insisted on doing her own lithographic work. The printer would deliver huge zinc plates, the size of four finished pages, and she would draw her illustrations directly on to them, one for each of the three primary colours and black. Easy enough if you can see the finished drawing, but unimaginably difficult if you are working with black litho chalks on a grey surface and having to make up the colours in your mind, all the time keeping them in register. Later the printers developed fine sheets of transparent plastic with a roughened surface which helped

with the register, but she still needed to work with black chalks and imagine the colour combinations she was creating. The process wasn't helped by the chalks, which were made of wax and softened unmanageably in warm weather. Keeping them in the fridge was partially successful, but in the end she was limited to working in autumn and winter.

'Tinkle was me, a much softened and more charming me. I was a complete rebel against the smug respectability of Didsbury where we lived'

When I first went to see Kathleen again, I was expecting to find a dreamy, rather fey woman in her early eighties. Instead I was faced with an astoundingly alert ninety-five-year-old, with a sharp wit and an impish sense of humour who had just written her autobiography. Her father had died, heavily in debt, when she was only five, leaving her mother to fend for the three children. Kathleen was farmed out to grandparents and an aunt before the family was reunited in Manchester when she was nine. It was an unsettling time. Was the idealised cat-family life of the books an attempt to recreate what she had missed in those years?

'Of course. And by the middle of the war when five had already been published I was always hoping that the evacuee children would be helped by

Kathleen Hale portrait by Jane Bown

them. They must have felt very much as I did separated from their parents.' Unexpectedly, though, Pansy, Blanche and Tinkle were not simply herself, her sister and her brother. 'No, Tinkle was me. It was a much softened and more charming me. I was a complete rebel against the smug respectability of Didsbury where we lived. I refused to do my lessons at school and spent most of my nine years there in the corridor in disgrace. But I lived for my drawing and the worst punishment my mother could give me was to take away my drawing things. Once I was nearly expelled for drawing bare-breasted mermaids round the margins of my scripture book but the headmistress overlooked it.' The same headmistress recognised Kathleen's ability and entered her for an art scholarship at Reading University College, which, to the annoyance of her contemporaries, 'the worst girl in the school' won.

After art school she came to London and joined the land-army in 1918, driving heavy horses from Barnes to Covent Garden daily. More material for the Orlando books, as it later turned out. Living on a shoestring in London she became part of the 1920s bohemia, somehow floating along on the lifebuoy of her remarkable talent. A chance meeting and a moment's banter with Augustus John landed her a job as his assistant and a long friendship.

Until recently, like most people, I was quite unaware of the outstanding quality of her other work. Did she feel any regrets that she had hung her 'slender reputation on the broad shoulders of a eunuch cat', as her friend Cedric Morris once put it? 'Those cats! Once I had done two books they became so real to me that they were in charge. I had a certain amount of control over them but they were always escaping. I would like to be remembered for my serious work but somehow Orlando took over.'

Well, Kathleen, it should be some consolation to know that you've given great pleasure to thousands of children over two generations.

Kathleen Hale died in 2000 aged 101

Brief encounters

NIGEL FOUNTAIN *looks at the lives of others*

Sean and I are drinking tea in an Uxbridge Road café west of Shepherds Bush Common, down from the London BBC Television Centre, talking about his friend Brian and about his mother. Sean looked after her until he was twenty-two. 'My mum,' he says, 'she smoked like – well, she was a chain-smoker.'

Sean is fifty-six, silver-haired, wide-eyed, slightly dishevelled, with a leather jacket and a green open-necked shirt. He was born in Waterford in the Irish Republic but when he was two, his father, who was a sailor, died, and his mother, looking for work, came to London. There were sixteen in her family but five died at birth. 'There are three sisters still in Ireland,' he says. 'You've got a lot of aunts,' I say. He laughs, and puts more sugar in his tea.

> **A *few years later Sean had a break-down. 'I didn't want to be dependent. I took an overdose. I thought I wasn't coping. I wanted to die'***

He went to school in Ladbroke Grove. 'I never had to learn anything,' he says. 'All I had to learn was my name and address. I never took any exams, it was too complicated. I left school at fifteen. I wanted to be a nurse. I wanted to be a fireman. Then I stayed and looked after my mum. Maisie was a compulsive bingo player, every day and every night. She loved bingo, she knew the people, and one night when she was sick at the hall, the people took her to our front door and they said, "Your mum is not well". I was there the day she died. She had just had her breakfast, went back to bed and her chest collapsed. My mum was young, sixty-one. I depended on her for everything,' he says. 'I've had a mental problem since she died. I adored Maisie, yes, I adored her.'

It was 1977 and his brother's girlfriend objected to Sean staying with them. He was trying to get the points for a council flat. An acquaintance told him about a room. 'He said, "Go to that hotel, Sean." I was there for six years, in one room. I had one friend who came to see me and to say, "Are you all right?" and we would watch my little telly. I got very friendly with the manager – I had to pay him £50 a

week and I was only getting £65 benefit. He would lend me £10 at a time. I got into debt. It was Earls Court, noisy, lots of Australians, Iraqis, lots of gay men and lots of prostitutes. I am a gay man. I was going into gay bars, trying to be friendly, and to make friends.'

In the early 1980s, he met Brian, an actor. 'I am not denying that he stayed overnight,' says Sean. 'It was too late to go home.' Three weeks later Brian rang and invited him over for a meal at his place in Shepherds Bush. They became friends, and in the late 1980s he moved in with him. A few years later Sean had a breakdown. 'He was good to me and I didn't want to take advantage, be dependent. I took an overdose. I thought I wasn't coping. I wanted to die.'

That was bloody stupid, I say, Brian would have been devastated. Yes, says Sean, as if it hadn't happened yet, and that he would be. 'He called an ambulance and I was in hospital for two weeks. I would never do it again.'

They lived together until 1996, and holidayed in Brian's flat in Spain. 'He used to help me all the time,' says Sean, 'and I helped him, and I did the shopping. He was my partner. He loved me.' Sean repeats that twice. 'I loved him – in a caring way. I only got interested in the theatre because of Brian, and he loved opera. I'd never seen opera in my life, but I loved it, especially *Turandot* and *Tosca*.'

The council flat came through in 1996 and Brian helped him move in and, from their two homes, they stayed together. But around that time Brian began to get shaky; Sean found he was helping him get up the stairs. By 2010 he had been diagnosed with advanced Parkinson's and moved into a home in Chiswick. 'That broke my heart,' says Sean. 'The home is not the same as going in our own front doors, letting myself in and out. I can't do that now. He's got carers, they are nice to me, but I haven't seen him so much, he's got other friends who go and see him.'

Sean says that he is happy, he will never leave London, but it is not like it was when he was with Brian. Brian's mind is intact but he is very ill now. Sean had wanted to tell somebody this story. 'Twenty-eight years I was with him. I did stand by him. I did.'

Sean finishes his tea. 'I adored Brian,' he says. 'I adored Brian, to this day.'

Death without the sting

For medical students, the dissection room is a place where gallows humour is honed and lasting friendships formed – and despite the move towards computer-based teaching, there is no better way of learning anatomy, says **JOHN McGARRY**

The very first dead person I ever saw was in 1956 when entering the dissecting room at Bristol Medical School. I and the three other students allocated this body referred to him as Yorick, but we soon changed this to Percy when we realised that all the other students in the room were also calling their bodies Yorick. After the initial distaste was overcome, dissection became a pleasurable collegiate exercise with chat to fellows on the other side of the lead-covered table leading to lifelong friendships and mastery of the art of gallows humour.

Each Thursday we had a viva on the previous week's dissection. I usually got As and Bs, but on 26th July 1956 I was rewarded with an E, as the day before I had joined a student demonstration in the centre of Bristol and was involved with setting fire to a Union flag as a protest against the impending British invasion of Suez. For this misdemeanour I spent the night in Bridewell's historic cells and was released without charge the following day in time to sit the viva. At the end of the course I was awarded an anatomy prize, and eventually became a surgeon.

Unfortunately, only a small number of medical schools still practise human body practical dissection – these days, most medical students learn anatomy on computers, which does not enable them to appreciate the feel of the organs. Bristol Medical School is one of the few which still does, and now, aged 75 and probably with not very long to live, in gratitude for my anatomical training all those years ago I have decided to leave my own body to them.

For this to be arranged one needs to write to their Bequest Office and complete a simple form. Like most people of my age, certain parts of my

After dissection is complete the largest parts left for burial are two eighteen-inch long femurs, so a much smaller coffin can be used...

body are no longer extant; but this is complemented by most organs being duplicated. So I have an absent knee and hip (replaced by prostheses), no foreskin (my mother was Jewish), and about two inches of vas deferens. The Bequest Office has been told of this, as well as my impending cataract operation.

Squaring the decision with my wife and four children proved a little delicate, and a discussion ensued with the local vicar as there would be no body available for a funeral service. He assured me that this was no problem – a memorial service could be held, followed by an interment when the body was returned. It was pointed out that this would be in three to five years time, and that there might only be a

few parts, as I had signed to allow any organs to be retained for future study.

After dissection is complete the largest parts left for burial are two eighteen-inch long femurs, so a much smaller coffin and burial plot can be used. The cleric was not amused by my request for a half-price funeral at the appropriate time.

Medical schools offer cremation, but this would produce carbon dioxide and dioxins, and I have no wish to contribute any more to climate change. Although I am a militant Dawkins atheist, I wish to be buried in the parish where I have lived in the former Rectory for more than forty years. Instructions have been given that my coffin should also contain a radio tuned to Radio 4 with a spare set of batteries (just in case). My wife refuses to erect a tombstone as I am not a believer, but suggests a small tree for the churchyard, or a plaque on the church wall.

Abdominal surgeons and anatomists will tell you that the one thing that makes their work much more difficult, and in the case of surgeons, more hazardous, is an excess of fat. So I have decided to diet towards my death. This is the first time in the world's literature that this dietary regime has been proclaimed – appropriately I am writing this on Good Friday.

ILLUSTRATION BY MARTIN HONEYSETT

Left to right: Julia Somerville, Annabel Hayter, Jon Snow, Jean Marsh, Terry Wogan, Barry Humphries and June Spencer in 2011

The **Oldie** of the Year AWARDS

The Oldie of the Year Awards have been held at Simpson's-in-the-Strand every year since 1993. Irreverent, unusual and damn good fun, they're hosted by the inimitable Terry Wogan and aim to honour oldies in every field – from politicians (past winners have included John Major, Vince Cable, Chris Mullin and Boris Johnson) and actors (Joanna Lumley, Eric Sykes, Tom Courtenay and Anne Reid) to adventurers (Ranulph Fiennes, Robin Knox-Johnston and Roger Allsopp) and campaigners (Marjorie Wallace and Terry Pratchett). Memorable awards include Carol Thatcher's 'Ball Cruncher of the Year' in 2006, Andrew Sachs as 'Grandad of the Year' in 2009, Liz Smith's 'Royle of the Year' in 2007 and Mary Beard's 'Pin-up of the Year' in 2013. Not forgetting our royal winners: Camilla, Duchess of Cornwall, won 'Spouse of the Year' in 2006, Prince Philip won 'Consort of the Year in 2011', and Queen Elizabeth the Queen Mother won 'Oldie of the Century' in 2001.

This page, clockwise from top right: **Richard Ingrams and Sir Terry Wogan, Ian Paisley, Tom Courtenay, Beryl Bainbridge and John Mortimer, P D James, Peregrine Worsthorne, Fauja Singh, Baroness Trumpington and John Major**

The Oldie

Buy it before you snuff it!

Above, from left: Tony Benn, Mary Berry, Ken Loach, Leslie Phillips and Peter O'Toole, Michael Heseltine, Anna Ford and Kate Adie, Maureen Lipman and Joan Bakewell. *Middle rows, clockwise from left:* Mary Beard receives her award from Sir Terry Wogan, Ronnie Corbett and June Whitfield, Roy Hudd, Melvyn Bragg, Jon Snow, Larry Adler on harmonica and Humphrey Lyttelton on trumpet, Peter Bowles and Kate Adie. *Bottom, from left:* Andrew Neil, Joanna Lumley, Ken Clarke, Prince Philip's acceptance letter

SANDRINGHAM HOUSE

I much appreciate your invitation to receive an 'Oldie of the Year Award'. There is nothing like it for morale to be reminded that the years are passing – ever more quickly – and that bits are beginning to drop off the ancient frame. But it is nice to be remembered at all.

I regret not being able to receive the Award in person, but I will not be conveniently in reach of London at the time. I hope the party at Simpsons will be a great success.

Rum customs

Local lore in Gascony dictates that to be treated with any semblance of courtesy, you simply have to know Terry Wogan. **PAUL PICKERING** *reports*

Condom. A very pretty town in Gascony, south of the Dordogne but more or less untroubled by the braying hordes of Volvo gypsies from the English home counties. Condom. Men move from foot to foot and try to whisper the name as in an old-fashioned barber's, forgetting to put the stress on the last syllable. Women are inclined either to look at their shoes,

or giggle. When asked where they are going for their summer holidays most people of the Tunbridge Wells sort cannot quite get their quivering lips around the pride of Gascony, Condom.

I too was a Condom virgin until I answered an ad in a Sunday newspaper and, after an hour or so's gentle drive from Toulouse airport, we discovered a paradise of a farmhouse below a vineyard in rolling Oxfordshire countryside. Except, unlike Oxfordshire,

it was both warm and totally empty. The only other house was about a mile away, at the other side of fields of sunflowers. Inside were oak beams and a wood-burning stove, and Evelyn Waugh and Graham Greene on the bookshelf. Outside, the spring-fed swimming pool was immaculate. Fruit trees ringed the house. 'I know the key worked. But do you think we've got the wrong place, or that it's haunted or something?' said my wife, with true British optimism. Just then I heard a cry from our five-year-old daughter, Persephone, who had wandered back into the garden.

'Daddy, it's Bambi,' she shouted as the deer, three does and a fawn headed off into the rows of vines. I grabbed her, tucked her under my arm, and we tried to follow. 'Where have they gone, Daddy?' Breathless, I stupidly said that the deer ran away because the locals hunted them. I then told her what hunting was. That was a mistake. Persephone wondered aloud, amid tears, why we had gone to a place where people were cruel to Bambi. *La Chasse*, everything from mushrooms to wild

JUNE AND GERALD by NAF

It would be nice to hear you use the 'L' word now and again, Gerald.

You're right, June, I should use it more. I'm sorry.

Lesbians. There, I've said it.

boar, is a minor religion in the area. The grandest shop in the centre of Condom proper, overlooking the river Baïse, had everything possible to exterminate wildlife. So I decided on a river trip.

We hired a motor-boat. I had just passed my Royal Yachting Association Day Skipper's exam in England and, with an insouciant wave to the very attractive lady who rented the boat, and the scowls of my wife and daughter, I roared off. Along the bank old men looked up from their games of boules and began either to laugh or wave in equal measure. 'Why are those men waving, Daddy?' I waved back with the calm assurance of the nation who won the Battle of Trafalgar. I then glanced in front of me. As we went under the bridge there was something wrong with the river. I had recently lost an eye and, in order to get perspective, had been told to go through a Stevie

'Why are those men waving?' I waved back with the calm assurance of the nation who won Trafalgar

Wonder routine of turning my head from side to side. But the roaring noise should have given the game away. 'Turn the boat round. It's a weir, you idiot,' shouted my wife. I could see the tops of the perch poles of the men fishing in the brook below. We just managed to get back to the main channel. 'That was good,' said Persephone. 'Can we do that again, Daddy?'

You can probably imagine the general merriment on the dock. Until about six in the evening most Condom residents go about in a shaky sort of stupor, recovering from the night before. After this they are drunk. The only things that rouse them from the

stupor are when a tourist tries to drive a boat over a weir, hunting, or the production of foie gras, where whole fields of ducks stagger around, bumping into each other like the men on the boules piste. 'Why are those ducks sick, Daddy? Are they going to be hunted?' Most of the poor things did not look as if they could walk, let alone run away. 'We force-feed them,' said Madame Terreblanche. 'Would you like some Armagnac? A tin of foie gras?'

We declined. Anyway, the tinned variety is just like Tesco's pâté. But once you taste the raw stuff, pan-fried in the finest butter with a surround of caramelised apples, you understand why the Romans invented sclerosis farming, and not just for the beastliness.

La Terrauboise restaurant was only a couple of miles from our house. 'You look like the German actor, Rutger Hauer,' said one of the three late-middle-aged Parisian homosexuals who ran the place and stalked the clientèle. 'Is your foie gras good? You know the actor I mean? The one in *Blade Runner*? He had a bad eye like yours. All bloody. You really should cover it with a patch when you go out to dinner. Are you an actor? You don't look like a writer. Perhaps you can sign our book...?' My jaw had more or less dropped onto my plate at the sheer venom. Persephone watched closely, pondering if this was anything to do with hunting or eating sick ducks. My wife kicked me under the table.

I signed the book and, to my surprise, noticed a name three lines above. 'Thanks for another great meal. We'll be back.' The signatory was Terry Wogan. 'You know Terry Wogan?' said the man who had handed me the book. There was another kick from my wife. I nodded. The mood suddenly changed. 'He is a great man in British television. He has a house down the road. He is Mr Eurovision Song. He is a singer and an entertainer.' The words were delivered with the kind of solemnity one gets at a memorial service for a judge. 'My husband knows his secret,' said my wife. I nodded. We dined out splendidly nearly every night, the three partners outdoing themselves in a quest for T Wogan's great secret.

Ah, the countryside can be a cruel place. But in Condom Terry Wogan was our *préservatif*.

RANT

THERE WAS A TIME when, weather conditions permitting, you could sit on the seat at the station and have a few minutes' quiet meditation waiting for the train. Not any longer. The announcements are nowadays non-stop. 'The train approaching Platform Two is not scheduled to stop here. Please stand well back on the platform.' Trains never stop at Platform Two because it's on the fast line, so there's never anyone standing on Platform Two. But you can't be too careful.

'We regret that the 8.42 service to London is delayed by approximately twenty-six minutes. We apologise for the inconvenience caused to your journey today.'

Step on the train when it finally arrives. 'First Great Western welcomes you on board this service to London. Please take a moment to read the safety instructions which are available in Braille on request.' As we approach the terminus, 'Please take care when alighting from the train. On behalf of myself and the onboard crew, we look forward to seeing you again.'

Step onto the platform: 'In the interests of safety, cycling and skateboarding are not allowed in the station... Please be aware that opportunist thieves operate at this station. Do not become a victim of crime... Unattended luggage is likely to cause a security alert. It can be taken away and destroyed.'

On and on it goes. How on earth did we manage in the old days?
RICHARD INGRAMS

ILLUSTRATION BY TOM PLANT

That was the BBC news

When **SALLY HOLLOWAY** *beat 399 other applicants to the job and joined the BBC as a radio reporter in 1951, recording equipment was basic to say the least...*

Kate Adie was definite and defiant when she stood in recently for Jimmy Young on Radio Two. 'Yes,' she asserted, 'I am sexist and I am a feminist.' Which surprised me because in my time as a staff reporter for BBC News we'd have probably been sacked for admitting to prejudice in any area – particularly sexism or feminism. A BBC reporter in those days had to be totally impartial – provided that the impartiality trundled along strict BBC lines.

But then so many things have changed since that era when the earth moved and 'Auntie' decided to advertise for a woman reporter. In 1951 they had lost Audrey Russell to the world of freelancing. She had joined the news team during the Second World War, after stage managing in the theatre and service as an auxiliary firewoman. The Beeb then decided to advertise for a trained and experienced female journalist. I – and some 399 others – applied. After a somewhat comic series of tests (including being sent to report a Sherlock Holmes exhibition in Baker Street, after which more than half the hopefuls had been eliminated for assuming that Holmes was the author), I got the job. I started in September 1951 – by which time I'd had nearly eleven years reporting with the Press Association and later the old *News Chronicle*.

There was no training school for radio news, although it was a very different medium from writing for print. Television news was still in its foetal stages. Microphones were huge and nicknamed 'frying pans'. Recording was a major operation – not surprisingly, as the tape recorder existed only as a rumour (of a hush-hush gadget invented during the war).

If the listener heard interviewees 'in voice' it was all down to the work of specialist engineers in recording cars. You could tell these huge black Humber limos were official by their green sun visors inscribed 'BBC Recording Service' in gold. (It was considered good manners to fold the visors up out of sight if we called at a fish and chip shop on the way back from an assignment.)

Breakdowns were hardly surprising. The back seat of each car was stripped out and replaced by two solid recording decks for 78 rpm discs while the boot was filled with batteries to power the equipment. On location the driver/recording engineer crouched over the decks, aided by an RPA (Recorded Programme Assistant) and the reporter told him when to lower the needle onto the acetate surface – and when to lift it. After a long session the car floor would be crunchy with swarf – the black threads of acetate cut from the grooves. Editing involved a soft yellow pencil to mark the place on the disc at which to start

'We'd like to start our Happy Hour, sir, if you'd please leave...'

Garden. Later he would return to rejoice or lick his wounds in the BBC Club before, sufficiently tanked up, he disappeared into the Langham (then a labyrinthine outpost of the BBC), soon to emerge on the foot-wide stone parapet which ran around the building at roof level. As startled drivers dodged breath-holding pedestrians in Langham Place, he would totter unsteadily along the stonework until he found an open window to fall into and sleep off the incident.

But there were others based in Egton House, the minuscule annexe of Broadcasting House which held News Division. Doug Willis, Valentine Selsey, Ivor Jones and Bernard Forbes were all first-class reporters, dedicated (with the occasional misgivings) to the BBC's principles of scrupulously impartial and objective reporting.

House rules demanded that anyone interviewing a minister should submit a list of questions in advance for approval, and then not deviate from them. The Royal Family (usually strictly the province of the Court Correspondent, Godfrey Talbot) were to be treated with the utmost discretion, deference and respect, as were all representatives of the Churches of England or Rome. When George VI was ill I remember including 'Marina blue' and 'Gloucester green' in a report on a new colour dictionary – and being accused of 'mentioning the Royal Family in a frivolous context at a time of national anxiety'. Another roasting came when I described a mediaeval mural of a Madonna as 'prim-lipped'. It might, I was assured, give offence to Roman Catholics.

I was already having withdrawal symptoms for Fleet Street.

Bernard Forbes had just disappeared off to the Ally Pally to help develop TV news; and we were humping round the first cumbersome reel-to-reel tape recorders when I left in 1954, too pregnant to get within range of the studio microphones. Listening to and viewing radio and TV news now, it's hard to believe how cut-throat competition, state-of-the-art equipment and satellite transmission have revolutionised the way news is presented.

Come to that, the rest of the world has changed a bit too.

playing the insert, and when to stop. In programmes such as the nightly Home and Overseas Radio Newsreels, which demanded quick reactions, you just prayed that the studio technician would find the right yellow dots.

By modern standards, News Division was a small unit, although many of the famous war commentators had already formed its basis, among them Thomas Cadette, the Hon

endless eruptions between him and the Head of News, Tahu Hole, a stolid and worthy New Zealander (known, inevitably, as 'Hole and Perfect').

Hole hit the roof when, allegedly against the terms of his contract, Cutforth published a book on the Korean War, which he'd been reporting for the BBC, in which he frequently slagged high ranking US Army officers for 'bugging out' when the going got

Microphones were huge and nicknamed 'frying pans', while recording was a major operation – the tape recorder existed only as a rumour

Edward Ward, Colin Wills, Doug Willis, Frank Gillard, Godfrey Talbot and Wynford Vaughan-Thomas.

They were often personalities but more charismatic than most was René Cutforth. René existed in a world of journalism epitomised by Evelyn Waugh in his 1930s novel *Scoop*. He specialised in wars and his view was not always that of his employers. Consequently there were

too hot. Hole and the hierarchy were livid, but René was too good to sack. When there wasn't a war in the offing he was quite capable of starting his own affray. This was usually after one of his lady friends had flown in from some faraway country to renew an old acquaintanceship. He would flee to drown his anxiety, ending around 4.30am in one of the small-hours-opening pubs of the old Covent

LEFT: Turning a blind eye?
Greek Street, 1973
BELOW: As fat as a fiddle –
Kenneth Drury at Bow Street
Magistrates Court, 1976
BOTTOM: Jimmy and Rusty
Humphreys, 1977

Partners in crime

There have always been rotten apples in the police, but never such a brazen
bunch as the bumper crop fielded by the Met in the Sixties and Seventies.
DUNCAN CAMPBELL *looks back on the golden age of corruption*

Commander Ken Drury, the head of the Flying Squad, had been putting on weight. All those lunches at the Caprice, all those dinners at the Savoy, all those tempting gateau trolleys. And all paid for by Britain's leading pornographer, the dapper and urbane Jimmy Humphreys. What to be done? Humphreys to the rescue, this time with the gift of a rowing machine and an exercise bicycle to get the commander fit enough to pick up those fat weekly bribes he was receiving for turning a blind eye to all the illegal smut of Soho.

This was London in the late Sixties and early Seventies, when bent police officers were in their pomp. In those days, the corrupt copper felt entitled to all the dancing girls and used fivers that the criminal world could throw at him, in contrast to today's much more secretive and – let's be fair –

very much rarer forms of police dishonesty uncovered in the wake of the Murdoch empire's phone-hacking scandal.

One major source of revenue in those days, for both criminals and police, was pornography, then a grey area of illegality still waiting for the waves of 'the permissive society' to wash away restrictive laws. At the centre of it was Jimmy Humphreys, 'the emperor of porn' or 'the Caesar of Soho' – depending on which newspaper's contrived nickname you fancied. With his attractive and vivacious wife, Rusty – a former stripper from Kent, whose ambitious mum had once hoped she would become Britain's answer to Shirley Temple – Humphreys built up a porn empire based on a handful of Soho clubs.

Soon he was made aware by detectives that, if he wanted to continue in business, he would have to buy them 'a drink' on a regular basis: 'a drink' being anything from a tenner to, in the case of senior officers, a couple of grand a month – plus a Christmas bonus. In this, Humphreys had learned the ropes from his mentor, Bernie Silver, a previous 'emperor of Soho', who had made a fortune from brothels and strip joints. He taught Humphreys the golden rule with detectives: 'get 'em young', then you could rely on them as they moved up the promotion ladder.

Humphreys, who died a few years ago, used to recall how he would have to take detectives and their wives for meals at the Ritz or Savoy and pick up the bill. Sometimes the wives expected a little something, too. On one occasion, a detective returned the gift of a necklace – not because of a guilty conscience, but because his wife's neck was too thick for it and he wanted a larger one. If the police were about to raid one of their bookshops, Humphreys would receive a phone call the night before with the advice 'Be like W H Smith' – i.e. get rid of all but a couple of porn books.

Commander Drury even felt relaxed enough to take a holiday in Cyprus with Jimmy and Rusty, something that even the most cocky of bent officers would never consider today. Alas for Drury, the *Sunday People* was on to his case by then and he found himself on a slippery slope that ended with a dawn raid, a blanket-over-the-head arrest, an Old Bailey trial and jail for eight years in 1977. He was perhaps the most blatant example of how corrupt the detective side of Scotland Yard had become, but lots of them were at it.

On one occasion a detective returned a necklace – not because of a guilty conscience, but because his wife's neck was too thick and he wanted a bigger one

Detective chief superintendent Bill Moody was the head of the Obscene Publications Squad, or 'the Dirty Squad' as it was presciently known at the time. He drove a Lancia and was on the payroll of both the Met and Humphreys. Moody – whose nickname was 'Wicked Bill' – and his superior, the debonair Commander Wally Virgo, one of the top detectives at the Yard, pocketed £53,000 between them in the course of sixteen months. No small sum in the early Seventies. Humphreys kept meticulous notes of his transactions and, when he was arrested on another matter, handed them all over to the anti-corruption police. Virgo and Moody were jailed for twelve years each, although Virgo was released on appeal and died a few years later. The straight-arrow officer leading the operation against corruption, assistant commissioner Gilbert Kelland, wrote later: 'The crow of corruption had to be nailed to the bar door.' Indeed.

Peter Scott, once Britain's most prolific cat-burglar and the subject of the 1965 film *He Who Rides a Tiger* (Tom Bell played him, Judi Dench his girlfriend Charles Crichton directed), knew Wally Virgo well. Scott now lives in a council flat in King's Cross, the proceeds from the odd Vermeer and Sophia Loren's diamonds long gone. He remembers Virgo and has his own theories as to why corruption was so rife then.

'Poor Wally,' he says. 'He was basically a straight-hand but when he saw that everyone else was in the pot, greed got

the better of him. I felt a bit sorry for him. In those days the wages for the police weren't that good and there was no fat pension to look forward to like there is now, so for someone like Wally to get £500 a month or whatever it was – it was just too tempting. I saw him after he was convicted. He couldn't look me in the eye – he'd reduced himself to my level.'

Not that corruption was confined to vice. One busy bank robber, Bobby King, who went on to take an Open University degree in prison and become an expert on the work of Virginia Woolf, described to me years ago what a simple world it was in the Seventies. 'I can't remember one local CID who wasn't crooked,' he said, explaining how every problem could be sorted by a bribe, from driving while disqualified (£25) to assaulting a policeman, possession of a firearm, assaulting the police (£2000, which included the officer explaining his own injuries to a magistrate – 'I could have fell in the scuffle'). The etiquette was that, on being arrested, the criminal would ask the detective if 'something could be done'.

Charlie Richardson, the gangster who ended up getting 25 years at the Old Bailey for violence, fraud and extortion in 1967, said in his autobiography, *My Manor*, that 'the most lucrative, powerful and extensive protection racket ever to exist was administered by the Metropolitan police. It was a sort of taxation on crime... sometimes we would pay people to be "found" committing small crimes so that our friendly local protection racketeer in blue could have someone to arrest and look like he had been busy.'

There were, of course, some white knights in this sorry affair. Sir Robert Mark, the Met Commissioner who eventually cleaned up the Yard, described the CID over which he took charge as 'the most routinely corrupt organisation in London'. He initially encountered enormous resistance in his efforts to purge it and is remembered for his pithy aperçu that 'a good police force arrests more criminals than it employs'. During his commissionership, fifty officers were prosecuted and 478 left early.

Of course, there has been corruption before and since. The old music-hall song 'If You Want to Know the Time, Ask a Policeman' was based on a belief prevalent at the time that officers stole the watches off drunken toffs. But the days of rowing machines, hols with pornographers and of such routine untouchability have subsided, like one of Ken Drury's soufflés.

'Hold on while I Google "sin"'

East of Islington
The unusual life of Sam Taylor and friends

A debt of love

Fungus Friend was sure his charm would win over Ruth the debt collector

Very few people would turn to Fungus Friend for advice on fiscal management and Ruth at the Hard Nosed Debt Collection Agency in Glasgow was not one of them. For years her boss, Mr Nuckles, had made a sizeable fortune recovering outstanding debts from payment-shy borrowers, and they didn't get more outstanding than Fungus Friend's.

It usually didn't take him very long. A few phone calls from Mr Nuckles, peppered with barely veiled threats hinting at years of reconstructive surgery, invariably yielded a swift return. But agency policy had recently changed. The authorities had received several complaints and Mr Nuckles had agreed to adopt a more sensitive approach.

Unable to manage the task himself – he had his reputation to think of, after all – Mr Nuckles had handed several of the more challenging cases over to Ruth, a colleague with a soothing manner and a fondness for cats. Ruth was a woman who liked to use the power of persuasion to get her man – and Fungus Friend was very open to persuasion.

He was certainly very open to her twice weekly telephone calls. She was single, female, keen to talk (about him) and was paying for the call. Why not? Besides, compared to Mr Nuckles, who liked to rouse his debtors shortly after dawn, Ruth was considerate enough to wait until after lunch, by which time Fungus Friend had been able to consume the best part of a bottle of claret kindly supplied by somebody else.

It put him in the right frame of mind for one of their little chats, while a free trial subscription to the *FT* had given him a newly acquired insight into the global downturn – one he was keen to share. Money, he pronounced to Ruth when pressed on the finer details of his mounting debt, was a problem everywhere, a commodity

in increasingly short supply. He had decided therefore that Ruth should be concentrating less on his personal wealth, or lack of it, and more on his other assets. Of which, he was sure she would agree, there were many.

He had been rather surprised to hear, for instance, that she had not been aware of his celebrity status as a crooner and had promptly dispatched a CD with a signed photograph. She was touched, she said when they next spoke, particularly at his failure to pay the postage, which showed at least some attempt at economising.

Then there was his aptitude for dancing. He had occasionally considered charging for his services as a partner – after all, there were very few men of his acquaintance with quite his grasp of the cha-cha-cha. Ruth wondered if he might ever consider procuring a real job of some kind. True, there was a recession on and opportunities were scarce, but

from what she could see from his file, it appeared he had never felt the need to take up paid employment. For a man whose credit card debts were larger than her mortgage, she found this *laissez-faire* attitude quite alarming.

'I don't want to sound pushy,' she sighed one afternoon, 'but I've been

Ruth should concentrate less on his personal wealth and more on his other assets

calling you for two months and I need to know what your intentions are.' Fungus Friend said that he quite understood. After all, he didn't want her to feel he was stringing her along. He said he was keen to develop their relationship further, perhaps over dinner. Ruth thanked him for his kind offer and said she felt she had to be brutally honest. 'I really am only interested in you for your money,' she said. 'And you can't afford dinner.'

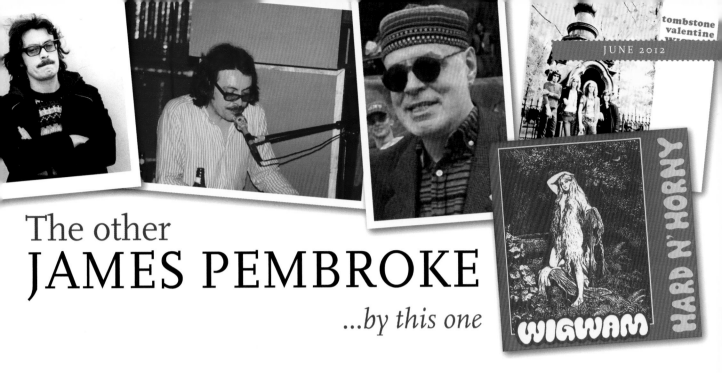

The other
JAMES PEMBROKE
...by this one

Google your own name at your peril: you may well end up drawing unfavourable comparisons with your alter ego, warns **JAMES PEMBROKE**

In 1994, under pressure from *The Oldie*'s aristocratic agony aunt, the Hon Ursula Wyndham, the editor asked me to investigate my lineage. Ursula, who was known to wander into drinks parties in her nightie and wellies, had become convinced that I was the Earl of Pembroke. (During a lunch I had told her a family legend that the Pembrokes were descended from one of Thomas Coram's original foundlings, who had been adopted by an eighteenth-century Earl of Pembroke.) Windsor Ancestry Research were only too happy to deprive me of my aristocratic pretensions by establishing a clear line back to William, a Deptford shipwright born in 1743, so predating the Foundling Hospital. Last year my cousin Stephen probed even further, only to discover that William's mother had given him the name Pembroke after one of her customers. She had other children to whom she gave different surnames, leading us to the obvious conclusion that she was a dockside prostitute, ill-trained in the arts of contraception. Much as I enjoyed the discovery, it has taught me to stay clear of digging round in my past.

But the internet, in the hands of children, can uncover many dead bodies one wishes had never been exhumed. Bored one evening, my own pair of internerds recently decided to google my full name. The name being relatively uncommon, the first page's search results for 'James Pembroke'

were largely about me. But there was another who had won a listing for himself in Wikipedia: 'James Francis (Jim) Pembroke, born 27th January 1946, is the vocalist of the Finnish progressive rock band, Wigwam,' I learned. At first perturbed by my rock star alter ego, I soon became fascinated by him. Twenty years my senior but no relation, he has enjoyed a far more illustrious career. Like his contemporaries, the Kinks, Jim had grown up in north London suburbia. Unlike Ray Davies, who was to sing of sunsets over Waterloo, our Jim followed his Finnish girlfriend back to her homeland in 1965.

In the wake of Beatlemania, Jim found himself in massive demand in Finland. Any young long-haired Brit clutching a guitar might have met the same reception in Sixties Helsinki, but he quickly formed the Pems (I had wanted that name for my own pop group when I was ten) before joining

*Top: the quietly dignified, relaxed and indubitably cool Jim Pembroke
Below: this James Pembroke, visibly haunted by his namesake*

Blues Section, with whom he recorded 'a blues-jazz-pop fusion album now considered seminal in Finnish rock'. In 1969, he joined Wigwam as their lead singer, and has been their frontman and principal songwriter ever since.

My daughter quickly went to Google images to make a physical comparison with her now weary dad. Raven-haired Jim dominates the album covers, evincing a quiet dignity in his grey ponytail and Marquess of Bath Indian jacket. But it's his solo career which most resembles the spoof 'rockumentary' *This Is Spinal Tap*. That there may have been 'artistic differences' between Jim and the other members of Wigwam is hardly surprising when one discovers what he got up to when left to his own devices. He released *Hard 'n' Horny* in 1969 and *Tombstone Valentine* the following year. Under the pseudonym Hot Thumbs O'Riley he released *Wicked Ivory* in 1972, followed by *Pigworm* in 1974. Clearly under the influence, he brought out other solo albums throughout the Seventies, including *Corporal Cauliflower's Mental Function*.

Although I'm sure we have nothing in common, not least his taste in music, I can't help harbouring a strong desire to meet the only other extant James Pembroke. Sharing a name must give us something to talk about, even if he 'Jimmed' his James. And he looks so enviably happy and relaxed. He's begun to haunt me. I'll even admit to looking into flights to Helsinki.

The **rains** came

Seething armies of ants devour anything in their paths and monster worms emerge from the swamps. **DONALD MACINTOSH** *describes the rainy season in the White Man's Grave*

Illustrated by PAUL HOGARTH

You know the rains are over when the bush cherries come into season. Slender stems of trees, barely three inches in diameter, suddenly sprout clusters of berries. They look more like clusters of green frog spawn in the permanent gloom of the tall trees, and even when they ripen to a gleaming scarlet hue, ready for eating, they don't look much like cherries.

Cherry season in November is my favourite time in the tropics, the equivalent of spring in the temperate zone. There is an excitement in the air, a stirring of life, a freshness and warmth after the chill and the wet and the numbing ennui of the rains. The storms may still boom over the pygmy forests of central Africa, but in the coastal forests of the White Man's Grave the skies are suddenly blue and cloudless. But from May to October, it rains and it rains. For six long months Mother Africa hardly ever closes the sluice gates.

It begins innocuously enough. The first rumbles come from over the sea far to the south, a faint low growling sound, inaudible to those who live deep in the forest and barely audible to those who live by the sea. It doesn't last long. The growling soon subsides to little more than a discontented muttering, fading into nothing as the storm takes itself off over the vast hot wastes of the Gulf of Guinea.

There is a lull for a couple of days, then it starts up again. A gun-metal grey wash of colour on the horizon widens almost imperceptibly, fitfully illuminated by the faint flickerings of an electric storm fretting over the water. The growling becomes progressively louder as the sapphire cloak of the sea is replaced by a mantle of sullen, liquid lead, and the dry, burning orb of the sun is transformed into a harsh, watery glare. There is an oppressiveness in the air, a brooding, suffocating heat. When the sudden breeze that presages the storm hits the land at last, it is almost with a sense of relief that the people of the Coast settle down to await the arrival of the rains.

The first storms are at their most dramatic in the forest interior. Clattering bursts of thunder shake the earth with their violence, and lightning flares and sears and splits the heavens in a continuous brilliance of cold yellows and greens beyond the dark of the trees. These first storms bring with them a wind that flurries and swirls and shrieks through the forest in demonic rage, and cause real damage. Great trees are incinerated by lightning bolts, others are uprooted and flung aside by the wind. On hillsides and exposed river banks, swathes are blasted through the forest, forming morasses of fallen trees and thorny vines.

But the ferocity of those early storms soon fades. As suddenly as they started, they stop. The forest settles down to the humdrum monotony of the rain season proper. The air is still and the rain comes down in a relentless torrent, so heavy that it is often impossible to see more than ten yards ahead.

Only foolishness or hunger makes anyone venture outside during these months. Main roads become little better than ploughed tracks, blocked by abandoned vehicles, and rivers become completely impassable. Water levels rise ten feet overnight, and rivers that had been as quiet as English chalk streams one day become roaring torrents the next.

The Owena in Nigeria is one such river. During the rain season it is transformed into a thundering, rolling brown flood that stops for nothing. After the Second World War, here and there along its course, bridges were built across the Owena to a standard design: abutments and piers were monoliths of stone and concrete, each pier being fifteen feet long by five feet wide, and tall enough to ensure clearance above the river at its optimum rain season height. For double security, each pier was bolted into the bedrock of the river. Spanning the piers were great baulks of ironwood, three feet

square, and, nailed to the tops of those beams with six-inch nails, the heavy plank decking and running strips required for the bridge surface. Until the season of 1957, I felt sure that nothing the elements could hurl at them could have inflicted the slightest damage.

That year produced the heaviest rains for many decades on the Coast. I was working in the forests of the northern reaches of the Owena, and the end of one day found me in a Land Rover churning

It was impossible to see whether the bridge still existed beneath the fast-flowing torrent of brown water. It shuddered violently under our wheels

its way south through seas of mud to our first bridge crossing. We reached it and stopped, thunder-struck. The river, heavily swollen when we had crossed it four hours earlier, had risen a further eight feet and was now rolling over the topmost planks of the bridge surface. Stuck behind the bridge was the most incredible assortment of debris: log ends, tree limbs, great piles of bushes festooned with liane, pit-sawn planks, an upturned canoe, a massive okwen tree, jammed firmly behind one of the piers. Its huge branches hung high over the bridge and the body of a drowned cow was wedged on top of them.

I would happily have gone straight back up the road and lodged in the timber camp for the night, but my driver was made of sterner stuff. He put the vehicle into gear and moved slowly towards the river.

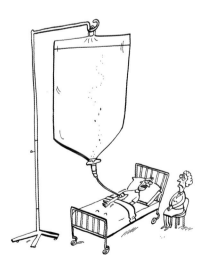

'The nurse doesn't come round very often'

Most of the decking was under a fast-flowing torrent of brown water, and it was impossible to see whether the bridge still existed beneath it. All the driver could do was to keep his gaze riveted on the point on the opposite bank at which he could just discern the top of the bridge abutment rising above the water, and drive straight towards it. With heart-stopping slowness, he did just that, the bridge shuddering violently under our wheels.

Several lifespans later, a collection of naked urchins standing in the bucketing rain raised a cheer as we pulled up alongside them on the far bank. My driver switched off the engine and lit a cigarette with shaking fingers.

We watched for ten minutes while the waters rose higher and the death groans of the bridge increased in volume. Finally, with one almighty crack, it was gone. Two great concrete piers went tumbling end over end downstream, and ironwood beams weighing several tons each were swept off like matchsticks.

If one had to travel in the rain season, it was better to do so on foot. My legs were my transport and the forest was my home. My life was governed by what was known as 'Africa Time'. If it was impossible for me to get from A to B today, there was always tomorrow. If a river proved impassable and there was no canoe to ferry me across, what of it? The obvious solution was to wait until the waters subsided.

I was no more fond of the rains than the next man, but I got used to them. My work cataloguing tree species went on throughout the year and I never made the slightest attempt to stay dry when out working: waterproof clothing would have been too hot and cumbersome for the amount of walking I had to do, and the condensation within would have nullified the whole point of the exercise.

There were some advantages to working in the rain. One got closer to the wildlife. Sometimes, too close. The relentless downpour seemed to have the same brain-deadening effect on wild creatures that it had on human beings. Trudging along a forest path with my eyes on the ground and the rain battering down, I have found myself having close encounters with buffalo, and in the midst of herds of bush pig and giant forest hog.

Some of the less obvious inhabitants of the forest claim the attention most in the rain season. Because of his

No one has ever travelled through the African rainforest without coming into contact with the driver ant. The first hint of thunder coincides with the start of mass movements over the forest floor by those voracious creatures. They are universally feared, and every able-bodied thing moves quickly out of their path. Driver ants figure prominently in

even injured elephants, being reduced to skeletons in short order. Their bite is ferocious, and any unfortunate unable to escape is eaten alive. Even when you pull them off you, the body comes away from the head, while their pincers remain buried deep in your flesh.

They are particularly active at night, and they are a horrible nuisance to those who have to sleep in the forest during the rains. Moving camp in the middle of the night in bucketing rain, with everything in the vicinity a seething mass of ants, is not for the faint of heart.

There are occasional lulls in the downpour, and these are the times that you remember with the greatest pleasure. You wake one morning to the sound of chimpanzees hooting and screaming their delight as a hazy sun breaks through the clouds and the mist drifts slowly through the branches of the forest giants like puffs of silvery cotton candy.

The first hint of thunder coincides with the start of mass movements over the forest floor by the voracious driver ant. They are universally feared

love of the rain and watery places, the rhinoceros viper is known as the River Jack. He is extraordinarily beautiful, patterned in a striking array of reds and yellows and greens and blues and blacks. He is surprisingly difficult to see on the forest floor. He has a filthy temper, and his strike is lethal.

The African earthworm goes on tour at this time of year, too. The first time I saw this harmless invertebrate writhing down the path towards me, all six slimy feet of it, and one inch thick from beginning to end, I experienced a thrill of horror. I stepped aside and watched as it humped its way blindly past me, moving with surprising speed and agility down the thin runnel of water which flowed along the centre of the path.

Swamp life comes into its own during the rains. Waters that have stagnated during the dry season are revitalised and spawn a new generation of life. Stirring in the murky depths will be the lungfish, an unprepossessing, eel-like creature which hibernates during the dry season in a nest of mud deep down in the swamp. When the water eventually rises and softens the mud enough to enable it to burrow its way back out, it returns to the waters of the swamp.

Swamps are the breeding ground of the malarial mosquito. The onset of the rains sees a rise in the level of the swamps and a consequent increase in the mosquito population. The male is a completely harmless nectar drinker: it is the female of the species that does the damage. West African mosquitoes can shove their needles through denim, and, in addition to transmitting three different types of malaria, they carry such fatal diseases as yellow fever and elephantiasis.

the folklore of the Coast, one popular belief being that before swallowing its victim, the python will always travel in a wide circle around it to ensure that the dreaded driver ants are not in the vicinity and liable to come upon it as it lies comatose after its meal.

The drivers move in columns, flanked by soldiers. The soldiers are formidable warriors: jet-black, about an inch long, with fearsome pincers on their jaws. Millions of them go on the march at any one time, in seemingly endless columns, little more than a few inches wide. Excessively heavy rain seems to disorientate them, however, scattering them in the surrounding bush, and the unwary traveller may suddenly find himself in a seething mass with no apparent means of escape. The answer is to run like hell with a high-stepping gait, stamping the feet hard on the ground as you go to prevent them from getting a purchase.

Among some tribes the ants are regarded as a blessing. They are the finest pest-control agency in Africa. Huts are abandoned until the ant hordes have passed through, by which time not a single rat, lizard, roach or flea remains. Nothing escapes their attentions.

But there are plenty of horror stories about tethered goats, cows in labour,

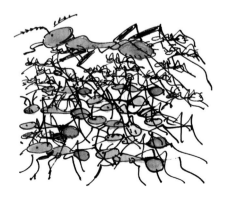

But these are rare interludes, soon to become a distant memory as the rain comes down again. Once more, you edge your way over rotting tree trunks spanning raging rivers, or flounder through endless swamps. Even when you reach relatively solid ground there is only the drumming of the rain in your ears as you squelch your way through the sodden forest. You are convinced that you will never be dry again and that this time, the rains are going to last forever...

And suddenly, as abruptly as it started, it is over. Once again the thunder rattles and clatters over the forests and lightning sears through the leaden clouds. But there is a subtle change in the atmosphere. The storms are drifting back to the mangrove swamps of the coastal lagoons. For a few days they will bluster and bellow, but every inhabitant of the Coast knows that this is the end. In a short time the skies will once again be blue and cloudless as the dry season returns to the Coast.

The emergent sun will bring new life to the wetness of the woods. For the next few months the treetops will ring to the songs of the birds and the chattering of monkeys, and the forest will become, once more, a paradise of perfume and colour. The cherries are the harbingers of this resurgence of life.

Maesobotrya berteri, the scientists call it. To me, they will always be November cherries. I can taste them as I write this, and no fruit has tasted half as good.

Unwrecked England

Rudston, Yorkshire

Candida Lycett Green

Rudston is in the big, sweeping David Hockney country of the East Riding. Stately trees, wide verges and well-rounded, may-choked hedges edge the road from Bridlington as it winds along the shallow valley of the Gypsey Race, the only surface stream in the Yorkshire Wolds. You could easily miss the village, most of which lies sheltered near the Race but, set a little apart, the church of All Saints with its fat Norman tower stands on top of a high knoll and is visible for miles around. Inside it is light and triple-aisled, with cream-washed walls, gold stars painted on the wooden ceiling (part of an extensive Victorian restoration) and a beautiful modern stained-glass window in the south transept depicting worshippers bringing fruits of the field to the Harvest Festival.

The huge churchyard which encircles All Saints has primroses among the gravestones, grand views of the Wolds in every direction, a gigantic dome-shaped beech tree and, near the north-east corner of the church, the most extraordinary and mysterious monolith I have ever seen. The late John Michell, *The Oldie*'s 'Orthodox Voice', made it a regular point of pilgrimage. Approximately 25 feet high, it is the tallest standing stone in Britain and is said to be buried as deep into the ground as it is high. The stone comes from Cayton Bay, about ten miles away, and was erected at this strategic point, above the dog-leg bend of the valley, millennia before the church was even thought of. Perhaps it was placed here to be at the heart of some ritually significant landscape: certainly the presence of four cursuses (Neolithic earthworks) nearby, as well as numerous earth banks, Bronze Age tracks and barrows, suggests that Rudston was an exceptionally important site to our prehistoric ancestors.

The Romans, followed by the Saxons, enjoyed the streamside site of Rudston and today it is reckoned to be the oldest continuously inhabited village in England. It feels settled and comfortable with its three-arched bridge over the Race, its post office and pub, its pantile-roofed, pinkish brick cottages, bungalows and sprinkling of modern villas lining the ancient ways. Off Long Street a short drive leads to Rudston House, the birthplace of the writer, feminist and social reformer Winifred Holtby. Her father was a prosperous local farmer and alderman while her mother became the first female alderman in Yorkshire. At Oxford, Winifred became a close and constant friend of fellow writer Vera Brittain. They later shared digs in London and when Vera married, Winifred moved in too.

Living in the shadow of mortality (having been diagnosed with the then fatal Bright's disease), she came back to her beloved childhood terrain to write her last novel, which is set here. Sarah Burton, the young headmistress and heroine of *South Riding*, is clearly Holtby's alter ego. She advocates social change and defends the right of single women to lead fruitful lives: 'I was born a spinster,' Sarah reminds herself, 'and my God, I'm going to spin.' Burton uncovers a local property scandal, a story-line loosely based on fact (Winifred admitted riffling through her mother's waste paper basket at Rudston to extract council papers). She died in September 1935 at the age of 37, soon after finishing the book. Vera, who was her literary executor, had to fight to get *South Riding* published the following year (Mrs Holtby tried to block it). The book has been in print ever since, and has been made into a film and two television series – another reason why Rudston has become a place of pilgrimage.

I was a Hackney looter

Raiding Woollies and thieving from market stalls – **DEREK JAMESON** *and his fellow waifs and strays in Ma Wren's Thirties slum knew all the tricks to a quick bob*

Illustrated by Peter Bailey

Harden your hearts. That cuddly toddler with the jet-black eyes plaintively demanding a handout is probably raking in a hundred grand a year for the folks back home in Bucharest. (Europe's gypsies long ago discovered there's money to be had on our streets for those bold enough to ask. The British have always been a soft touch.)

Perhaps that explains why the Scouting Association is reviving bob-a-job week, though this time around the campaign will be based on community projects rather than individual scouts knocking on doors offering to wash the car and mow the lawn. The service was suspended after forty years in 1992 because

of concerns about child protection (paedophiles, in other words).

Paedophiles certainly didn't worry us lot growing up at Ma Wren's. A few choice words and they would be off like frightened mice, though their tougher brethren manning barges down the road on the River Lea did

I was on hand as a 'shabbos goy' (sabbath gentile) to run errands or light a match. My aim was to light the fire badly in the hope that it would soon go out

feel entitled to a tanner's worth of our service – if they could catch us.

We operated our own help-thy-neighbour scheme at Ma Wren's gloomy Victorian slum in the hungry Thirties. Between the wars she raised

some seventy of us – waifs and strays growing up on the streets of Hackney. Ma was the prototype old woman who lived in a shoe. Her only income was her 10/6d (52½p) weekly widow's pension plus a few shillings now and again from the so-called fallen women whose misbegotten

progeny had landed in her lap. So it was a case of beg, borrow or steal, as she never failed to tell us, and that meant getting out there in search of money. I was a major contributor from the age of seven.

BRAVE NEW WORLD

Watch your step...

Our richest pickings came from theft. Something for nothing has always appealed to the poor, though there's a price to pay if caught, as today's rioters have discovered. We would grab and run with anything that moved and had a potential value, though we never robbed our own kind – the impoverished working class. A gang of us would raid Woollies – Woolworth's – or street markets and create mayhem, running like the clappers from yelling traders. Once I ran a mile clutching a twopenny comb with a salesgirl breathing down my neck.

Jewish immigrants escaping the pogroms made up much of the local population in those days. Harold Pinter's family lived down the road at Clapton Pond and Alan Sugar in a block of council flats off the high road. His family shopped at Charlton's the greengrocer, where I would crawl under the stalls to steal apples. We were perpetually hungry.

Orthodox Jews were not allowed to light fires or handle money on their Sabbath, beginning at dusk on Fridays, so I was on hand as a *shabbos goy* (sabbath gentile) to run errands or light a match to get around their religious scruples – Jewish enterprise! My aim was to light the fire badly in the hope it would soon go out. Foster-brother Len would be in the street outside awaiting a summons to have another go. Another sixpence in the kitty – a good earner in those days.

Money didn't always come that easily. Those were the days when there were more horses than cars at work in the streets. I would go around with an old bucket and shovel collecting horse manure. Next thing was to find a house with a decent-looking garden and hammer at the front door.

'Her y'are, Madam. Fresh today, lovely horse dung. Just right for your roses. Tanner a bucket.'

Most garden-lovers were only too pleased. A few would turn nasty. 'Git aht of it, you little guttersnipe, messing up my front step.' That was a good cue. Soon as they disappeared indoors, tip a load over the stoop.

Keep an eye open for repairs to tramlines on the main roads. Loads of wooden blocks covered in tar lying about – wonderful firewood at tup-pence a bundle. Careful, though, the night watchmen striking out with their heavy boots could leave you covered in bruises for weeks.

Uncle Sid was a good earner. Ma Wren's middle-aged son, he was totally demented. She reckoned that when he was young, hooligans buried him up to the neck at the seaside and it turned his brain. Sid collected empty milk bottles for Dick, a sympathetic United Dairies milkman, at a tanner a day. Trouble was, Sid had an obsession that kind souls trying to help him were stealing his money, and the day came when he hit Dick over the head with an empty milk bottle. The kindly milkman let it go, as did the local Congregational minister. Sid earned a few coppers on Sundays pumping the church organ – until he stormed out of the organ loft and clouted the vicar mid-sermon, demanding his money.

Rough, tough times. But we needed the money. Electricity was replacing gas in those days, but we often couldn't afford a penny for the meter. Frequently our only light was a halfpenny candle flickering in a cocoa tin as we sat in the gloom around the kitchen table, supping tea out of empty jam jars. The adults claimed the only china cups.

Christmas was a Dickensian nightmare and 75 years later fairy lights and other festive baubles still bring on the vapours. The only presents I recall ever receiving were a tangerine and a second-hand *Robinson Crusoe*. To this day it remains my favourite book.

Happy days? Of course. We never stopped laughing.

'Go get 'em tiger!'

THERE ARE some people who find our giant new shopping malls relaxing. Not the size of them, but the fact that they are ideal for a relatively anonymous spot of retail therapy. Such shoppers, however, may feel less relaxed about a new system that follows their every move through the signals on their mobile phone.

Not content with surveying everyone through closed circuit television, the owners of some of Britain's biggest malls have devised a new way of following their customers' movements. The FootPath system, which is in use in shopping centres in Bristol, Aberdeen, Portsmouth, Glasgow and Exeter, tracks every move you make. 'Discreet monitoring units' placed throughout the mall latch onto Temporary Mobile Subscriber Identifier (TMSI) signals which are randomly generated by a customer's mobile phone. The system collects the data and records the shopper's movements, noting which stores they visit and in which order. It also measures 'dwell time' – the length of time a customer stays in each shop.

The idea is to give retailers a closer view of shopper behaviour and improve the layout of their mall. This should help reduce bottlenecks and 'optimise staffing levels'. Path Intelligence, who invented FootPath, insist that they have no way of identifying individuals and do not have access to mobile numbers, messages, conversations or texts. They add that there are signs in each mall advising people that they are being monitored. But objectors, led by the civil liberties group Big Brother Watch, say the law needs to look again at the issues of privacy which mobile phone tracking systems raise. While FootPath may not store the personal details of mobile users, 'other technologies that would allow this are available'. There is, currently, only one sure-fire way of avoiding this particular level of surveillance. Switch your phone off.

JANE THYNNE

★ Great Bores of Today ★

Drawn by **MICHAEL HEATH**, words by **'FANT AND DICK'**

'...ladies and gentleman I know the hour is late and you're all of you anxious to get home some I know live a good couple of hours' drive away but I can't let you go without a word of thanks to a number of people and I am sure you won't mind if I single out Betty Jill and Tom who toiled tirelessly through the day to put this evening together and which I must say has been an outstanding success not just because of the work put in behind the scenes but to everyone here on whose sturdy shoulders our enterprise remains afloat if I might put it like that and I do apologise for our late start this evening due to a gremlin in the kitchen first and foremost I ask you to put your hands together for our chairman who unfortunately wasn't able to be with us but his good lady is here oh no she appears to have left but our treasurer is still in situ and I know would like just to say a few words...'

'...moving on from Shepherd's Bush this is where he moved to after Skinny Lizard saw Barking Black Jack at number one his flat was up there you can just see the window over that sign for Mario's Wood Oven Pizzas the front of this block has been completely rebuilt but the inside is more or less the same about this time he started going out with Lyn Gilkes who had been living with Dave Wattis lead guitarist of Last Orders who lived round the corner at 32a Old Beak Street if you go to the roof you can just see the Post Office Tower and he started writing the album Road to Atlantis which is inspired by the view and went gold in the summer of '71 then he split up with Lyn and he moved out to Swiss Cottage where he wrote Reverse Mirrors and the flat was taken over by Mick Nodes drummer of Red Mist who lived here three weeks before his tragic...'

'...the situation in Mali is complicated by the involvement of the breakaway Al Qaeda group Bafta Mouli which has now joined forces with the Jihadist movement in the north of the country led by the charismatic figure of Al Ghori once the sworn enemy of the PVFC who currently control large swathes of the desert areas formerly occupied by bands of hardcore Islamic Jihadists who are believed to have links with the Libya-based RMJQ the danger from the West's point of view is that these breakaway groups could now join forces with the powerful DVLC to establish a militant nucleus which could threaten the stability of the Eastern region round the capital of Monolulu currently controlled by elements of the moderate RSVP don't forget we're dealing with an area here twice the size of Mexico...'

'...help yourself to some marmalade I made it myself if you're interested I could give you my recipe it's well worth doing you can only get Seville oranges for a couple of weeks in January so you have to be quick off the mark I cut up the oranges into little strips then you simmer them for a couple of hours I used to wrap all the pips up in muslin but now you can buy special sugar with lots of pectin in it so it's easy to get a set it tastes so much better than anything you buy from the shop don't worry about that it's only a bit of mould...'

John Sweeney
ROVING REPORTER

Holy crap

The Kabbalah Centre is a scam and its founder a conman

FOUR THOUSAND years ago, a set of spiritual principles was communicated to humanity. These ancient revelations unlock all the mysteries of humanity; the secret code that governs the universe. This extraordinary powerful set of tools is the original instruction manual for life. Not my words, but those of the Kabbalah Centre, founded by the late Rabbi Philip Berg, who died in September 2013. It was his great achievement in life, some say, to bring the ancient truths of Judaic mysticism to a mass audience of believers.

Madonna, the most famous celebrity apostle for the Kabbalah Centre, mourned his passing with the following heartfelt tribute: 'I learned more from him than any human I have ever met.'

Back in 2005, colleagues at the BBC and I investigated the Kabbalah Centre. At the time, wearing the red string on your wrist and muttering gnomic stuff about the Zohar was all the rage. As well as Madonna, other celebrities who have reportedly had a brush with the Kabbalah Centre include David Beckham, Demi Moore, Britney Spears, Roseanne Barr, Ashton Kutcher, Mick Jagger, Jerry Hall, Naomi Campbell, Elizabeth Taylor and Paris Hilton.

One should not speak ill of the dead perhaps – unless you have spoken plainly about them when they were alive. In that light, I can say with confidence that Rabbi Berg was a conman and his 'extraordinary powerful set of tools' the spiritual equivalent of the horse-burger. The Kabbalah is a body of Judaic mystical texts, many of them written in Spain in the Middle Ages, which exist to be studied and which one should respect; the Kabbalah Centre is a scam, passing off New Age mumbo-jumbo as sacred learning in a movement memorably summed up by the American cult critic Rick Ross as 'Jewish Scientology'. I'm no rabbinical scholar, but I've met plenty of rabbis who say that Berg made a living out of fooling people. The story of Berg's confidence trick sheds fresh light on our dismal moronic celebrity culture, and how we confuse fame with wisdom.

Feivel Gruberger was born in 1927 in Brooklyn. He went to a Jewish school, was trained as a rabbi and then received a higher call – he became an insurance salesman. In the early 1970s he abandoned his first wife and seven children and set up shop as a Kabbalah scholar, giving himself a doctorate. Rabbi Eliezer Sandler told me that Berg had no right to do so: 'He had no PhD or anything like that. It's fishy, it sounds totally dishonest if I'm being kind, and brings into a question a lot of what he is doing.'

Ex-members of the Kabbalah Centre and relatives of loved ones inside it said it was a cult. One ex-Kabbalah Centre worker told me: 'You could call it brainwashing, but you are just in this state of mind where anything that contradicts whatever is said to you in the Kabbalah Centre just passes you by. You just don't get it, you don't hear it. You think that anyone who is trying to tell you otherwise, they are messengers of the devil, or the other side as they call it in the Kabbalah Centre, or they just don't know what they are talking about.'

This bleak view is backed by Rabbi Barry Marcus of London's Central Synagogue: 'There is very little difference between the way they operate and the other cults do with regard to sleep deprivation, exhaustion, keeping people very tightly bound and breaking the bonds with their family and making them totally dependent on the Centre itself. These are classic methods which are employed by many cults, especially with the pressure that they bring on some to break their family ties.'

The Centre sells healing Kabbalah water at £45 for twelve bottles. We discovered it came from a Canadian bottling plant which had been investigated

To find out whether the Kabbalah Centre was cash-driven, as ex-members said it was, we sent in a mole. She was told to come up with more money: from her parents, from her bank. One KC worker told her: 'This is the one time I tell people if you have to borrow, if you have to sell your TV or a piece of jewellery, it's worth it. Find a way. Take a credit card and borrow it. Borrow it from a friend meanwhile. If you have some knick-knacks, sell them and get some money from it.'

The Kabbalah Centre sold healing Kabbalah Water. We sent in Tony Donnelly, recently recovered from cancer, to find out more. At the Centre, he was told: 'The Kabbalah Water has strong healing powers. We have one girl who works here, her mother used to have cancer and she doesn't have it anymore because she drank the water. The water is very, very good because it affects the cells, it cleanses the cells.'

A case of twelve bottles of water cost £45, the Zohar book to go with it £289. We discovered the water came from a Canadian bottling plant which had been investigated by the local health authorities for impurities. Not that healing, then.

The Kabbalah Centre said: 'For millennia, Kabbalah has been misrepresented by people trying to discourage others from studying its wisdom.' Rick Ross was less polite: 'It caters to the narcissism of many celebrities; they want to have enlightenment, they want to be happy and they want people to cater it. Just like the catering trucks on location for their movies and their concert tours.'

'I recommend the fish again, sir'

'I've got sand everywhere'

The **Oldie** ON A DESERT ISLAND

'Oh... wow... is it...? No! It can't be!
But... wait... yes... yes! It is! Coconuts!'

'No, there's no one else here. Except Stephen Fry, of course'

'Are you paying too much
for your car insurance?'

Beth Chatto

Designer, plantswoman and author Beth Chatto is one of Britain's most influential gardeners. On her ninetieth birthday **DAVID WHEELER** *celebrated her career*

Britain excels in raising influential amateurs – a band of knowing, achieving and sometimes revolutionary individuals who, in all but a few fields, can leave many a trained academic on the starting blocks. When Beth Chatto hit ninety in 2013 the horticultural world was reminded of the profound garden-changing influences pioneered by one of Britain's greatest proponents – still active, though now at half speed.

Looking for someone of Beth's vintage who might have early recollections, I called on Ronald Blythe, who notched up his own ninetieth birthday in 2012. 'One day in the early 1960s,' he tells me, 'while visiting the artist John Nash, he said, "What do you think? Beth Chatto is going to make a garden at Elmstead Market and wants us to take a look at the site." So he and I drove to a track which was very like that to *his* garden at Wormingford, although on the level. And there was a gravel

pit – nothing else. She and I were old friends – or, rather, young friends – and I never doubted her abilities to do anything... Her guru – and mine – was the plantsman-artist Sir Cedric Morris, whose garden at Benton End, Hadleigh, was where we often met.'

My own adventures with Mrs Chatto began some twenty years later with possession of my first proper garden – a third of an acre on the Surrey/Hampshire border where the soil was little more than desert sand.

CLOCKWISE FROM LEFT: the Scree Garden, which includes five island beds, provides a home for many small plants that would be out of scale in the main Gravel Garden; Beth Chatto; the Water Garden; the Gravel Garden in high summer

I had a friendship during the last ten years of her life) and although the two women hadn't met for many years, Beth renewed their acquaintance in the 1970s while in London exhibiting at a Chelsea Flower Show where, it almost goes without saying, she scooped up top prizes for a decade

> " *A steady flow of Beth's inspired and inspiring books plus visits to her nursery and garden have taught me much of what I know and, more importantly, what I understand, about plants and gardens* "

It coincided with a book that Beth might have written specially for me: *The Dry Garden*. A few years later, living in mid Wales, where annual rainfall was quadrupled, I turned to its companion, *The Damp Garden*. A steady flow of inspired and inspiring books has followed ever since and these, plus visits to Beth's Essex nursery and garden, have taught me much of what I know and, more importantly, what I understand, about plants and gardens.

Another habitué at Benton End was the young Elizabeth David (with whom

or more. This renewal of friendship resulted in me driving the frail E.D. (she was born in 1913) to Beth's White Barn House on a blowy spring day when an east wind left Elizabeth tense with cold, but which the hardy B.C. considered no more than a balmy southern breeze.

In a long and dedicated life Beth has lectured in many parts of the world, making chums as easily as a willow makes roots. Her friendship with the late Christopher Lloyd was immortalised in *Dear Friend and Gardener*, a 1998 volume of plant-and-people chatty letters to and from each other. And that Sussex connection continues with Lloyd's 'right-hand man', Fergus Garrett, who describes Beth as one of life's 'great givers', likening her attitude to plants and people to a 'religious experience'.

Steven Wooster has photographed Beth's garden over many years. 'She was always supportive, and would let me know if I hadn't quite captured her vision, and that honest feedback was something I greatly appreciated.'

In 1987 Beth Chatto received the Royal Horticultural Society's highest award, the RHS Victoria Medal of Honour, a precursor to her appointment as OBE in 2002.

I still take every opportunity to see Beth's diverse acres. As Ronald Blythe blithely says, 'She made a unique garden – and a celebrated one.'

Many happy returns, Beth.

The Beth Chatto Gardens
Elmstead Market, Colchester CO7 7DB
Telephone 01206 822 007
For more information visit the website at www.bethchatto.co.uk

From Bow *to* Biennale

In the Twenties and Thirties a group of working men and women who learnt to paint at evening school achieved critical acclaim. **LAURA GASCOIGNE** *welcomes a new book telling the story of the largely forgotten East London Group*

rtists tend to gather together in schools, like fish, for self-preservation rather than instruction – an individual artist can sink without trace but a 'school' is less likely to be forgotten by history. The East London Group's misfortune, vis-à-vis history, may have been that it originated in an actual school. Whatever the reason, it was almost completely forgotten until David Buckman rescued it from oblivion in a fascinating and densely researched book, *From Bow to Biennale: Artists of the East London Group* (Francis Boutle, 2012).

In the mid-1920s a young Yorkshireman, John Cooper, fresh from the Slade, took over the art class at Bow and Bromley Evening Institute. Its members were working men and shop girls who thought art meant copying seed packets and photos of film stars – but by getting them to paint their surroundings instead, Cooper turned them into genuine artists. His star pupils were the window cleaner Albert Turpin, the engine driver Elwin Hawthorne, the plumber Archibald Hattemore, the basket maker Henry Silk and the Steggles brothers, Harold and Walter, both clerks. He even persuaded Walter Sickert to give a series of lectures, which made the shop girls giggle. 'Ha!' Sickert confronted one, 'You are laughing at my socks,' and pulled up a trouser leg to reveal a flash of crimson.

Sickert's support got the group its first public show at the Whitechapel Art Gallery in 1928, sponsored by Sir Joseph Duveen and Samuel Courtauld. It was such a critical success that the director of the Tate, Charles Aitken, arranged for a selection of works to transfer to Millbank, prompting the eye-catching headline 'Navvy Artist Hung'. But it was a series of shows at the Lefevre Gallery in the West End that sealed the group's artistic reputation. With the opening of the 1930 exhibition by 'the decorative Labour MP' Lady Cynthia Mosley, as reported in the *Sketch*, the annual exhibitions became a fixture on the London arts circuit. The further decorative additions of two extremely pretty former Slade girls, Cooper's fiancée Phyllis Bray and Brynhild Parker, doubled the group's appeal to the popular press, but it also attracted serious critical attention. A reviewer in *Apollo* hailed the East Enders as 'the Douaniers Rousseau of London' who 'would – were they Frenchmen and, preferably, dead – already command high prices'.

The apogee was reached with the inclusion in the 1936 Venice Biennale of Elwin Hawthorne's *Una Via di*

Cooper's star pupils were a window cleaner, an engine driver, a plumber and a basket maker

Londra and Walter Steggles's *Scena Presso Chichester*, before the war blew everything apart. Bombed out of his London flat, Cooper retreated to Yorkshire with a nervous breakdown and died in 1943 aged 48. Of his former students, only Walter Steggles and Albert Turpin persevered with painting the changing face of the post-war East End – Turpin fitting it in between other commitments to window cleaning, Moral Re-Armament and, from 1946 to 1947, the Mayoralty of Bethnal Green.

Buckman has pieced together an extraordinary story. All that's needed now is an exhibition at the Whitechapel and a feature film directed by Ken Loach.

Facing page: teacher John Cooper's *The Great Ventriloquist* (1930) and Albert Turpin's *Sally (Mum)* (1925) This page, top to bottom: *Thorpe Bay*, (Henry Silk, 1933); *Cumberland Market* (Elwin Hawthorne, 1931); *Marian Square, Hackney* (Albert Turpin, 1952)

Joan and her nutters

*When he was a little boy, London cabbie **PAUL BIRD** used to hang around the bombsites of West Ham with his mates. Their lives were changed when they were befriended by the theatre director Joan Littlewood...*

Illustrated by PETER BAILEY

I was born in West Ham on 18th July 1958 and until the age of ten I lived on a small street called Salway Road. My house was an end-of-terrace property with a shop-like front, and came with an outside bog and inside tin bath. It was later demolished under the Slum Clearance Act, but it wasn't a slum, it was my home!

Just across the road stood the Theatre Royal Stratford East, and adjacent to this was a street called Angel Lane which ran from Stratford Broadway to just past the theatre stage door. Angel Lane was a typical market street with little shops on both sides. Market stalls and barrows lined the street with traders shouting and yelling, selling their wares. You could buy anything – fruit and veg, fish, eggs, stockings, knickers, men's pants, dog food – you name it, you could get it.

Next to my house was a bombsite, and on the opposite side of the road was a smaller bombsite full of rubbish and weeds. These wastelands were our playgrounds. We would play and dig holes and tunnels in search of treasure. We would often find old coins and scrap metal and go home filthy dirty but rich. We did all the other stuff, like upsetting the neighbours with games of 'knock down Ginger', and hanging about on street corners in general. Like most

kids we got bored easily. But all that changed when we came across Joan Littlewood and her Theatre Workshop.

We were loitering on the corner of the smaller bombsite, and out of nowhere this strange woman, wearing a light blue merchant seaman's cap, approached us. She introduced herself as Joan and started asking questions. 'What's your name? How old are you? What are you doing? Why are you hanging about on street corners?' She had a very calming voice and, although very inquisitive, she had a kind manner about her, and seemed really interested in us.

She turned to her assistant, Christine. 'Can't we do something for these kids? Can't we get this place cleaned up, get them involved, and get them doing something?'

Christine nodded in agreement, and within weeks things did happen. We started to get the place cleaned up. Everyone got involved, including local residents. Joan got onto the council and we got planning permission to turn the site into a play

One day it was arranged for me and another kid called Paul Prendergast to meet the theatre's pianist. We were always bashing about on the piano and Joan thought we needed lessons, so this young musician was ordered to give them. We were taught the basics then shown exercises to practise in our spare time. The musician was Carl Davis.

Town, to my favourite restaurant.'

'What food we having?'

'Chinese,' she replied.

China Town? Blimey, the furthest we'd ever been was to Canning Town! China seemed a long way to go, and what was Chinese food? We soon found out, and about twenty of us piled into this restaurant in Limehouse. None of us had ever been to a restaurant, and none us had ever sampled foreign food. We loved every minute of our exotic experience and, yet again, Joan picked up the tab.

Joan had a pet name for us – she called us her 'nutters'. I can't work out why, but she did. It would be my nutters this, my nutters that, and so on. It wasn't to offend, it was a term of endearment. Even years later, she would write letters to me and refer to her 'nutters' and how she missed them. She went on to tell me how talented, bright and alive we were and that she'd back our gang against Eton!

Come the cold winter nights, Joan would let us into the theatre, but we had to stay quiet and behave ourselves. We would sit up in the gods and Joan would be up there too, scribbling notes on her clipboard

area. We got a lot of help from local tradesmen and building companies. Christine would flutter her eyelashes and all sorts of things came our way for free – gloves, picks, shovels, paint, sand, cement and lots more. We even got builders to come over and lay slabs and put down flat concrete surfaces of all different colours, giving us perfect play areas.

Come the cold winter nights, Joan would let us into the theatre, but we had to stay quiet and behave ourselves. We would sit up in the gods and Joan would be up there too, scribbling notes on her clipboard. She did this without looking, her eyes and ears fixed on the stage. We saw the shows so many times, we knew the lines and the words to the songs. (My favourite productions were *The Projector* and *Mrs Wilson's Diary*.) We got to know the cast members too, and after rehearsals Joan would get the actors to do little sketches with us, getting us to improvise and have a bit of fun on stage.

After Joan's death, a special appreciation night was arranged at the National Film Theatre. As I took my seat I bumped into one of the actors who used to play-act with us, and not only did he recognise me, but he remembered my name. I couldn't believe it after forty years! He recalled how Joan would make him and his fellow actors act out these little sketches with us. It was an order. In fact, everyone working in the theatre – electricians, carpenters, wardrobe and scenery workers, etc. – was told to give up a little time to teach us things about their trades. I don't think they were happy about this – after all, they had a job to do, didn't they?

Joan always had time for us, and she was very generous. We used to visit her office most days to say hello and have a chat. It was a small room at the top of the theatre, just outside the upper circle, and had a low ceiling which you could reach up and touch. Joan would be there working away and smoking French cigarettes, but she would always break off to talk. We were standing there talking one day, and all of a sudden Joan shouted, 'Look at your shoes. You can't walk around like that.' We looked down at the kid standing next to me and his toes were poking out. Joan shook her head and gave him two pounds and said 'For Christ's sake, go and get some new shoes.'

Even when she was under pressure or stressed she'd still have time for us. Well, almost. Once, we went up to see her, and she was really stressed. In a very kind way, she told us to 'Sod off and play somewhere else'. But having said that, she smiled at us, gave us five bob and told us to get an ice cream.

One Sunday she decided to take us all to lunch. 'We're going to China

In 1968 my house in Salway Road was demolished, just like everything else around it. Only the theatre was saved, thank God. I moved to a new house and lost contact with the theatre and Joan. She carried on until Gerry Raffles's death in 1975.

I never forgot those wonderful times. One evening in 1994 I watched *Omnibus* on BBC television, and there she was, in my front room. What a shock. All those years and she was still around. I had to make contact. I wrote a letter to her and sent it to the BBC to pass on. She received it and we kept in contact by letter for years. I also arranged a reunion and got hold of a few nutters from the past. We made a date to meet at one of Joan's favourite restaurants. We all arrived together including Christine. Joan loved it. It was a complete surprise – Christine had managed to get her down to Soho for the night and the nutters were there. She couldn't believe it.

Joan died on 20th September 2002. I was invited, along with other nutters, to attend her funeral. It was probably the best funeral that I'd ever been to. Joan's order of the day was quite simple. No priests, no vicars, no hymns, no religion – just fun and laughter. And we certainly got it.

I will never forget Joan and what she brought to us: the arts, culture and my love for the theatre.

Joan Littlewood RIP.

'How many times must I tell you? Stop drawing on the bloody walls!'

On Route 66

Left: Wigwam Village, Holbrook, Arizona *Right*: Elvis's bedroom in the Tradewinds Motel, Clinton, Arizona
Below: the Blue Swallow Motel, Tucumcari, New Mexico

HANK WANGFORD *and son journey back in time on a road trip down Main Street, America*

Steinbeck called it the Mother Road in *The Grapes of Wrath* and it stuck. Bobby Troup told us to get our kicks on it and we still do today. It's the America that escaped from the corporate maw. At 2,448 miles, Route 66 is the longest, thinnest neighbourhood in the world. People have friends hundreds of miles each way, from Chicago to Los Angeles. Since the Twenties it has taken dreamers and refugees to the land of milk and honey. It is The Way West. Great tracts of it are still there.

Driving across the rolling Oklahoma prairies, my son Mat's van started overheating. We cruised gingerly through Tulsa, past signs for Broken Arrow, Mustang and the Chisholm Trail. Yukon, Oklahoma, said 'Home of Garth Brooks' on the water tower. We drove on. No time for New Country.

Mat looked for some Stars and Stripes items – a hat, T-shirt, anything to make us anonymous, part of Middle America. Warned me not to cuss or swear. These are God-fearing folks who don't tolerate 'Well fuck me sideways' like

the British. 'Jesus Christ, Dad,' he said, 'don't say "Jesus Christ". Round here they say "Cheese 'n' Crackers".'

The Tradewinds Motel in Clinton, Oklahoma, a Sixties classic, sits on Route 66. Built by a retired vet, it was Elvis Presley's favourite. Halfway between Memphis and Las Vegas, the King stayed here four times. We stopped there on July 4th. The office walls were covered with 66 wallpaper – Chevys, cactuses, motels and all. 'I guess the Elvis suite is booked out for months?' I asked forlornly. Nope. It was free. What? Independence Day, and Elvis's bedroom is *free*? Did the world's Elvis Fan Clubs know of this?

The retired vet, now in his late eighties, told us about Elvis's visits here. The first three times, the Cadillac caravan arrived at dead of night and Elvis stayed holed up in room 215 with his boys next door ordering room service until, burgered up and ready to rock, they slipped off again. No one saw them and Doc was sworn to secrecy. The fourth time, the housekeeper delivering meals saw the King through the door and ran through Clinton spreading the news. Townsfolk gathered below the balcony. Elvis came down and played ball with kids in the parking lot then drove off and never came back. Room 215 has been a shrine ever since, with the original kingsize bed, vanity table, daybed and bathroom fittings from Elvis's days.

I'd always been frustrated by Graceland's pious refusal to allow us upstairs to see Elvis's bedroom or lavatory, a place too holy for us ordinary folk – 'That's where Elvis passed on.' Well, eat your heart out Memphis, Clinton's the place to be. Better than Graceland, we could *sleep in Elvis's bed,* sit on his very toilet.

The room is a multi-textured pentagon. Two angled walls are bare brick. One is wood, two others have red drapes. Matching dark red bedspread and drapes complement the purple carpet with squishy three-inch underlay to break any fall. The furnishings are a ragbag of eras, Sixties mixed with French Royal repro. (Wasn't it Louis XIV who favoured the white Formica marbled effect with the gold edging?) The Sixties are cherished with white leather bowl armchairs and a stripper's black vinyl casting-couch with a buttoned S-curved back which slides out on railway lines. Mat was sure that's where Elvis would have had sex: 'No, not in the bed, honey. C'mon, that's where I *sleep*.'

On the other side of the road is the Oklahoma Route 66 Museum. It tells the story of the Mother Road decade by decade, from Thirties dust bowl Model T Fords through Seventies hippy-flowered microbuses. The curator told us of

PHOTOS COURTESY © ION ARNOLD IMAGES LTD / ALAMY, JOHN NORRIS AND 3030VISION

fifteen hundred Harley riders rumbling past the week before.

The van had recovered in Elvis's parking spot. The 'Check Engine' light went off. Elvis heals in wondrous ways. He guided us to Jiggs, another of Clinton's treasures, a smokehouse full of truckers eating bunloads of barbecued pork, where we bought a bag of the best and cheapest jerky (sun-dried beef, cowboys' staple road food) anywhere in the States.

Elvis stayed with us. Kept us cool. Temperature in the nineties but no overheating. By Sayre it was 100 degrees outside Beckham County Courthouse, featured in *The Grapes of Wrath*.

Erick is a dusty one-intersection town, home of King of the Road Roger Miller. The West starts here. We rolled through under the big skies, grain elevators poking out of the flatness like missile silos. We high-tailed it across the Texas panhandle, kissing a sliver of the Blarney stone in a hunk of green concrete in Shamrock and marvelling at Groom's wonky water tower – the Leaning Tower of Texas. Hot winds welcomed us to the high Staked Plains.

We stopped at the Big Texan on the edge of Amarillo for a tea-time steak. Inside we met a New Jersey madman who was running the entire length of Route 66, repeating the foot-flattening Bunion Derby of 1928. Twenty miles a day in the maddening desert heat.

But then Elvis abandoned us bigtime. After our steaks we found Mat's van had been smashed into and everything I had – passport, money and credit cards, clothes and cameras – had been stolen. All I had was what I stood up in. No identification. I was the Man with No Name.

Stripped of any identity, things were refreshingly simple. No options – no worries. We headed for the safe haven of the Blue Swallow Motel in Tucumcari, blue neon under a full moon, another sweet piece of Forties timewarp full of 66 memorabilia. Neighbourhood pals of the Big Texan, they took care of us after our smack in the face.

Stretches of 66 rise and fall like a sleepy switchback inches away from the Interstate which slices through the landscape with its thundering cargo of 18-wheelers. It feels like driving through the Forties with the future ribboning alongside.

Grants, New Mexico, a mining ghost town, had a uranium mining boom in the Fifties. Its legacy is a series of Korean-owned motels, ours the astro-turfed Leisure Lodge. Mile-long freight trains rumbled through the night under the full moon. Grants' jewel is the beguiling Uranium Café where we sat on mauve leatherette banquettes under a mauve ceiling and gobbled nuclear breakfast burritos served by born-again Christians.

A couple of days on down 66 an old man with a Swap-Meet (car boot sale) in the roasting New Mexico desert put a smile back on my face. Tom Lamance, 87, had sat there for

sixteen years in a roadside shack surrounded by junk and hubcaps. 'Came here in '85. Used to be an auctioneer. Guess I kept more 'n I sold.' Outside in the fierce sun thousands of hubcaps dazzled and blazed. One in a distant row called me. I got to it and found 'GP' in the centre. We were heading for Joshua Tree, Gram Parsons's last resting place. It was befriending Gram in 1970 that caused my messianic derailment into the emotional world of Country music. A cosmic coincidence? Tom told me it was from a Seventies Pontiac Grand Prix. My blood froze. Twenty-five years ago I drove down 66 past here in a... Pontiac Grand Prix. After sixteen years in the desert, Tom had become a shaman and was doing a Castaneda on me. Back in the hippie days we called it fucking with my mind.

Stretches of 66 rise and fall inches away from the Interstate with its cargo of 18-wheelers. It feels like driving though the Forties with the future ribboning alongside

Another must-stay is El Rancho in Gallup, full-on Thirties Hollywood Western style. The film stars' favourite, with rooms dedicated to Gregory Peck, John Wayne and Ronald Reagan, it's full of chunky Wild West motifs, Navajo rugs and stagecoaches on the sofas. The lobby is a palatial log cabin film set. I was happy to stay in the John Wayne room, where the Duke luxuriated in two queen beds with wagon wheel headboards.

What finally wiped away my pain was the wacky Wigwam Village in Holbrook, Arizona, surrounded by the Painted Desert. Built in 1950, fifteen concrete wigwams have been lovingly restored. Classic cars sit outside the wigwams. Inside the bedroom is circular and *inclined*. Everyone should stay at least once in one of these concrete wigwams. They are at the heart of Route 66.

The Mother Road? Well, it was a mother to me. Main Street of America? Yep, I'll buy that too, even if it is the America of memories and dreams. What is America to us but the movies?

'...and once the same-sex marriage threat which created conflict between Church and state was resolved, the two princes were married and lived happily ever after'

Dickie Bird

picks his top six

1. Barbra Streisand
The greatest professional artist in the world. She has got a beautiful voice. I have got all her tapes. I would love to meet her.

2. Tommy Cooper
He was a great comedian. Also he was a tremendous character. They don't make comedians like him any more. He was the best. As soon as he walked on the stage he made you laugh.

3. Sir Garfield Sobers
The greatest all-round cricketer the world has ever seen. If there has been one better I would love to have seen him play. On top of that he was a wonderful gentleman, who played the game in the right spirit.

4. Princess Anne
She does a tremendous amount of work for charities. She goes about her job in a very quiet way, behind the scenes, unknown to people. She is a credit to the nation.

5. Mother Teresa
She did so much for the sick, the blind and the poor throughout the world. She was a wonderful lady whom I admired.

6. The Queen
She does a tremendous job, and she works very hard for our great nation. On top of that she is a wonderful lady. I am a Royalist.

PIN-UPS

PHOTO: REX

Left: Dickie Bird

Jeremy Lewis
LIVING HELL

Gripes and grumbles from The Oldie's resident sage

The pop singer Morrissey's *Autobiography* shot to the top of the bestseller lists after Penguin agreed to publish it as a Penguin Classic, and its gratified creator found himself rubbing shoulders with Montaigne and Machiavelli. Although the book received some good reviews, I instinctively sided with those who found it pretentious and long-winded. But my real grouse was with Penguin for so casually debasing the coinage, albeit in a highly profitable way. In an unexpected reversal of roles, the liberal-minded *Independent* accused Penguin of wrecking 'overnight the reputation of a global brand' in order to 'kowtow to the whims of a petulant pop icon', whereas the *Telegraph* saw the offence given as part of the joke, admired the author for pulling off an 'audacious literary heist', and praised his 'beautifully measured prose style'.

Allen Lane would not have been amused. He had left school at sixteen, and had founded Penguin Books in 1935 to make the best books available to the general public for the price of a packet of fags. He was in the high-minded but seemingly defunct tradition of educational self-improvement embodied in the Workers' Educational Association, the wartime Army Bureau of Current Affairs, and the Open University; and, shrewd businessman as he was, he always refused to take Penguin down-market. After his death in 1970, Pelican Books bit the dust (recently revived), and Pevsner's Buildings of England series was disposed of: as a publishing conglomerate, Penguin is no different to HarperCollins or Hachette or Random House, with whom it has merged, in that it happily publishes both bilge and classy goods (best embodied in the Allen Lane imprint, the most impressive publishing list in London). But Penguin Classics, founded in 1946 and the quintessence of what Lane himself stood for, was what differentiated it from its rivals – until Morrissey came along.

Shaving one's head to conceal premature baldness is understandable if misguided – baldness is a natural if wind-swept state of being, widely associated with an enviable virility – but the shaved head *per se* has a sinister, dehumanising quality, suggesting that the wearer sees himself as cold-blooded, robotic and inscrutable. Hairstyles, like clothes, are visual shorthands, touchingly indicative of how we like to present ourselves to the world at large. Whether dashing or grotesque, elegant or repellent, waist-length or crew-cut, they are part of our personalities; whereas a shaven head – like nudity, or the niqab – has an anti-social element, in that it reduces the extent to which we can 'read' its proprietor.

And whatever happened to the 'corrugated' look, as worn in the Fifties by Hugh Gaitskell and Benjamin Britten? I have always assumed that Gaitskell's hair scuppered his dreams of becoming Prime Minister, while Benj's crinkles almost certainly influenced my views on his music. And what about the widow's peak, once sported by such dapper coves as Dennis Price, Cary Grant and Allen Lane, but now a fading memory?

Yet another scheme has been launched to revitalise Battersea Power Station, out of action since 1983 and a husk of its former self: ingredients include a roof garden, viewing platforms on the rebuilt chimneys, luxury penthouses costing £30 million apiece and the inevitable shopping mall. It was designed by Giles Gilbert Scott, and is said to include art deco work, but why this crazed obsession with the old monstrosity, no doubt referred to as a national 'icon'? If one has to save defunct power stations, how much better to recycle, as planned, the Lots Road version, an elegant Edwardian construction a mile or so upstream on the other side of the

> ## I have always assumed that Gaitskell's corrugated hair scuppered his dreams of becoming Prime Minister

Thames. I've been aware of Battersea Power Station since 1947, when my parents moved into a flat on the south side of Battersea Park, but long familiarity has failed to induce waves of affectionate nostalgia. Bring on the wrecking balls, say I.

PS: Another of Scott's power stations was converted into the Tate Modern: given the stuff on display, a mixed blessing.

I used to enjoy listening to Radio 3 while shaving and eating my Grape-Nuts, but whereas until a year or two back the *Breakfast* programme consisted of some old boy putting on gramophone records of classical music, with occasional breaks for the news, the modern version is blighted by endless talk. Long-winded and self-important members of the public are not only encouraged to phone in with their views on particular pieces of music, but to text or email their thoughts on the most fatuous matters, few of which have anything to do with music: on 5th November, for example, the hapless Sara Mohr-Pietsch urged us to reveal how we liked to celebrate Guy Fawkes night, so unleashing a tidal wave of bores. Silence at the back of the class should be the order of the day.

85

Knock, knock. *Who's there?*

It's **DAEMIENNE SHEEHAN** *at a spiritualist demonstration...*

I had heard about the spiritualists from my hairdresser, who visited them on a whim one Saturday. Her visit was enviably dramatic. At the gathering, the spiritualist, named Billy, had chosen a young lady. 'Do you speak German?' he asked. 'Yes.' 'I don't quite know how to tell you this, but your grandfather was a Nazi.' Those assembled gasped. 'I had no idea,' the young woman blushed. There was an audible tsk from one member of the audience followed by, 'Of course she did.'

I decided to check out the cross-dimensionalists for myself. Since 1872 the Spiritualist Association of Great Britain has been pleasantly situated in a street of embassies in Belgravia, where it first gained the attention of Sir Arthur Conan Doyle, a great defender of the faith. Sedate and discreet, with a hall dedicated to the mystery writer, the Association also has a café offering reassuring mugs of tea for the post-epiphanised, and a chapel. The hour-long services were called demonstrations and cost four quid a shot. No latecomers were allowed: 'Service starts promptly on the hour.' Even when you were dead you had to be punctual.

The demonstration room looked like an old-fashioned Temperance Hall. We sat on wooden chairs facing a raised platform with the only comfortable seat in the room, an ornately carved wooden throne framed by dusty pink velvet curtains, like a roulette wheel at a game show.

We were a mixed lot. There were Spanish au pairs, a Belgravia matron and her dashing gentleman friend, a widowed builder, a traumatised spinster and a man suffering from writer's block. There was also an Aleister Crowley acolyte, wearing a crown of gold twinkly stars and waving a hawk's feather as he luxuriated within the folds of his Lurex cape. We were watched over by two watercolours of genteel elderly ladies who looked like Agatha Christie fans but were, in fact, 'guiding lights' in the spiritualist world.

Our contact with the other world was a large woman with little hands and a great deal of spring in her step. An ex-hairdresser from South London,

> **'I don't know how to tell you this, but your grandfather was a Nazi,' said the spiritualist**

her hair was cerise and her top fuchsia. She smiled at us benevolently, then asked us to shut our eyes to assist the spirits. Several of us peered around the room to see if anyone had followed the instructions. 'Or keep your eyes open, if you like,' the spiritualist boomed.

She began by telling us she felt our pain – a headache, to be exact. 'It's like a band of pain, coming from the right side of the room – does anyone on the right side of the room experience

headaches?' A small sad woman at the front stirred slightly. The spiritualist pounced. 'You're hard on yourself, aren't you?' she smiled in a big-sisterly way.

'I suppose I am,' came a tiny voice.

'Well, this spirit tells me you mustn't be too hard on yourself. You're about to make a big decision, but you mustn't rush it. Selling property, are you? You're doing a good job. It's a lady spirit, can you take her? Because if you can't take her I don't want you to force yourself. It may not be the spirit you're thinking of. Perhaps it's the gentleman behind you. Yes, it's your grandmother.'

'But I didn't really know my grandmother...' the widower said.

'Doesn't matter, she knew you,' our guide said brightly, pausing to explain to the rest of us that even if we didn't know the spirits, they could still help us.

'But...' the widower began again. The spiritualist moved on to the Belgravia matron. 'Are you about to make a major decision?'

'No,' she answered, unequivocally. 'Can someone else take that – it's an elderly woman who passed on recently. How about the lady in red? Good energy colour, red.'

'I need more information,' I said, feeling rather hot in my jacket.

'She had a fever, oh I feel it now, I'm all hot, I'll have to have a drink of water, oh I wish this was gin, no, just joking... She didn't walk that well. Tell me, are you confused about something?'

'Not really.'

'Did you know someone who passed on recently and had a problem walking, bless her?'

'I'm afraid not, sorry.'

She then approached the elderly gentleman at the back of the room. Dressed in black tails and white shirt, he was sitting poker-straight in the way that only the war generation are capable of. 'Oh ho ho,' he nodded amiably. 'Yes, I believe I can take her. That would be Violet.'

'She was a bit of a busybody, wasn't she?'

'Oh ho ho, yes, I suppose you could say that. Yes.'

'And she warned you, didn't she, to take care on slippery pavements, and now you've gone and injured yourself?'

The ramrod-straight veteran gazed at his plaster-cast arm. 'Yes, but I didn't listen,' he smiled to himself and Violet jubilantly.

The spiritualist turned now to the man with writer's block, who was also in the process of a major life-change. He took the advice easily, conceding that he had a tendency to let things go. She continued to make her way around the room. Conspicuously fair, she spent no more than five minutes with each person. Those most obviously in need, the timid and those weary with longing, were given extra time. She reminded me of a hen tending to her chicks. We waited to be drawn out, checking the clock surreptitiously in case the hour ended without our being picked. But she remembered every one of us.

The otherworldly therapy continued with the spiritualist predicting that one of the Spanish au pairs would ditch her boyfriend, and that the widower would take up dancing. Even when, at the end, Violet the Busybody's friend turned out to be a member of the Society, I found it hard to find fault. It was so childishly unbelievable. One might as well take offence at being told fairies were housekeeping at the bottom of the garden. Besides, hadn't we all gone away with a prize of sorts? For each person the spiritualist had something positive to impart. The only people she couldn't assist were me and the Aleister Crowley character, who left abruptly after she swore that a recently deceased cat had suddenly appeared in the aisle. His last words were, 'He was orange, not grey. I know that cat.' Then he sashayed out of the door, his feather waving like a maverick question mark.

Why had the rest of us stayed? My hairdresser had wanted the spirits to tell her to move to Dorking. I wanted to be ordered to write a book. The spinster was having doubts about selling her house. But it was the widower who seemed to get most out of the service. His wife had died of cancer a year back, and it was his fourth Saturday at the Association. He was at a loose end without her, and terribly lonely. Dancing, he thought, might be a wonderful way to get out and about again. Now he had permission.

MIND THE AGE GAP

Lizzie Enfield

'THANK GOODNESS they've gone!' was always the first thing my mother's father would say, after seeing visitors to the door. My father is not dissimilar.

'How long are you staying?' is usually the first question he asks when we pay him a visit.

If we answer 'Only an hour or so,' then he will sit down and chat. If we arrive at midday and say we're staying until six, he will carry on doing whatever he is doing, then come in and chat, then go to bed until we leave. If we present him with the woeful fact that we are staying the night, we may not see him at all.

I like to think it is not just the prospect of spending time with me and my family that sends him running for cover, but that it's a standard reaction to too much time spent in the company of just about anyone.

My mother is more sociable. She enjoys a visit, relishes a chance to chat and positively looks forward to a party.

My father, on the other hand, reacts to an invitation to a party, say in April, with the response 'But we went to a party last August'. He was like this in his forties but now he's in his eighties I can see that parties are harder – too much time spent standing up, plus the difficulties of not being able to remember who anyone is or hear what they are saying. As the festive season reached its conclusion, I could almost hear him breathe a sigh of relief – no danger of another invitation making its way through the letterbox for a few months, apart from the odd funeral.

Now that I am firmly in the midst of middle age I get invited to parties by people who are eligible for Saga insurance. These differ from parties given by younger people in two respects: people arrive early, and they leave early.

'Don't be fashionably late,' my father advised when I spoke to him on the telephone before setting off to one such party. 'Old people get there at the very start. There will be nothing left to drink if you get there hours later.'

Not wanting to be the first to arrive, I ignored his advice and got there half an hour late. If this had been a party given by one of my contemporaries, I would probably have been the first to arrive, but as it was full of oldies, the party was in full swing. I could hardly get though the door. I was the only one being given a glass rather than having mine topped up for the third time, and the canapés were already looking sorry for themselves. An hour or so later, people began to leave.

I'm at the age where friends no longer have to rush back for babysitters, so they tend to make the most of it, staying well beyond midnight and only leaving when the last drop of alcohol is drunk. This is not always great for the host but some are better than others at ignoring guests who won't leave. One of my relatives regularly leaves dinner guests sitting at the table and goes upstairs to sleep, telling them where to find more wine if they want it and to make sure the door is properly closed when they eventually go. She occasionally comes down in the morning to find one or two crashed out on her sofa, but appears not to mind. (I suppose going to bed when your guests appear intent on outstaying their welcome is the middle-aged equivalent of going to bed in the afternoon when your guests appear intent on staying till tea time.)

Of course if the party you are hosting is not actually in your house, then you can go home, leaving your guests to it. I attended one such party shortly after Christmas. It was the sort of party my dad thinks you need to be in at the start of, i.e. most of the guests were well into retirement. I got there not too late and left early enough not to be on the last train back to Brighton.

As I was looking for my coat in the designated coat-room, I heard the host come in with his wife. They did not see me lurking behind the coat rail. The host grabbed his coat and let out a groan. 'I think we've been here quite long enough,' he said. 'Let's get out of here!'

QUEEN MARY
and THE WOOLLY GIRLS

VERRALL DUNLOP *reveals how Queen Mary indulged her taste for fine fabrics in the days of postwar rationing*

In 1946 I became a 'Woolly Girl' at No 22 Bruton Street, a graceful, eighteenth-century Mayfair house where we organised exhibitions of wool cloth funded by the International Wool Secretariat representing the wool-producing Dominions – Australia, New Zealand and South Africa.

Our drawing-room floor was reached by a curving staircase tucked behind which was a very small lift. Go down and you were in the boiler room, go up and you reached the upper floors of the house. As we never used the lift, the exit to our floor was covered by a heavy wool draught excluder.

One day we heard the rumble of the lift stopping followed by the clanking of gates, and the curtain billowed forward to reveal the firmly corseted pale blue behind of a lady in a matching toque, accompanied by a surprised and rather agitated companion.

In a flash, our resourceful boss Patricia recognised Queen Mary, dropped a curtsy and welcomed her as though she had been expecting her at that very moment.

An imposing and upright figure, the Queen had spun round on her parasol to face the right way, but her lady-in-waiting emerged looking rather deflated and crumpled: unfamiliar with lifts, she had already taken Her Majesty down to the basement boiler room en route to the first floor. It seemed that they had both found this an interesting experience and they pronounced themselves proud of their achievement in reaching the destination unharmed. (At that period in her life Queen Mary suffered from not having enough to do, and seeing something reported in the paper, she would gather her faithful lady-

in-waiting and set off to investigate unannounced – as one could in those security-free days.)

The visit was a great success and was repeated on a regular basis. The fabrics were the main attraction for the Queen, who was renowned for her acquisitive ways. Grey wool lace was her particular favourite. Although clothes rationing was still in force, the manufacturers

always managed to find a length of anything she admired. Someone at Marlborough House would tip us the wink that HM was on her way, and a quick call to Moyses Stevens in Barclay Square would produce a bouquet in a matter of minutes. One girl stood ready at the front door, another at the lift to avoid trips to the boiler room, with Patricia to welcome at the gates.

Before long she knew all our names, and we enjoyed a near informal relationship with her until the big bosses from the Dominions got wind of the royal visits and wanted to be in on the act. Next time a visit was announced the chairman, a Dr Booth of Australia, arrived hot-foot. The lift gates clanked, Patricia dropped her curtsy and the royal presence stepped forth with her hand out to greet her hostess. This was too much for Dr Booth, who pushed in front of Patricia and announced in stentorian tones, 'I am Dr Booth, Chairman of the International Wool Secretariat'. Queen Mary was a great stickler for correct etiquette and this rotund little man had not been presented to her. She swept past him without a word and greeted the Woolly Girl whose turn it was to hold the door open. 'Good Morning Miss So and So, and how are you today?' Dr Booth might have been invisible, and forever after she referred to him as Dr Boots.

We had to move from our beloved Bruton Street to very modern offices in Dorland House. But that didn't deter Queen Mary, as our showroom, though less elegant, was bigger and better and there was even more to see. It was now the late 1940s and Dior's New Look was sweeping all before it. Never had there been a more exciting fashion moment after years of austerity and padded shoulders. The wholesale firm of Dereta fitted us all out with catwalk copies, and we fancied ourselves something rotten. One of us, Betty Frith, was particularly elegant. She had very dark hair and her New Look choice was stark unrelieved black – she looked like a fashionable crow. It was her day and mine to hold the door to greet HM inside the exhibition. The Queen acknowledged Betty, then, turning to me, said in a sympathetic whisper, 'I am so sorry to see Miss Frith is in mourning' – for a royal, the only reason to be dressed in black.
One day Queen Mary led me in to

a central stand where we could not be seen and surreptitiously brought out an envelope from her pocket. 'My child,' she said, 'could you do something for me?' 'Of course, Ma'am,' was my obvious reply. Out came a small cutting of beige tapestry wool. 'Could you

match this for me?' she asked, rather secretively. 'I am making a carpet and I have run out of background wool.' Patons & Baldwins duly obliged and delivered a great many of their distinctive pale brown flat boxes, which stood piled up at least knee-high. Immediately I went off to Marlborough House and put them into the hands of the lady-in-waiting. A month or so later the telephone rang and a well-modulated voice asked when the wool for the Queen's carpet was coming. I assured the lady-in-waiting that I would look into it, but boggled at the thought of

'Now watch your step, OK?'

having to ask Patons & Baldwins for more – no charge had been made for the first lot. The next day an apologetic call came from the lady-in-waiting: 'You will be pleased to hear we have FOUND the wool. It was in her LITTLE BOOT CUPBOARD.' She explained

The Queen was renowned for her acquisitive ways – grey wool lace was her favourite, and the manufacturers always managed to find a length of anything she admired

that the housekeeper had tidied away the boxes and then departed leaving no instructions, having had a stroke.
As a young man my grandfather had attended a lunch in Switzerland with the Tecks – known in those days as 'the poor Tecks' – an impoverished family who eventually made good by marrying their daughter May into the British Royal Family. My grandmother gave me a photograph of the lunch and I took it down to Marlborough House late one afternoon with a request that the Queen would be kind enough to sign it. To my surprise, before lunch the next day the photo came winging back, not only signed and dated but with a list of all the others in the photo.
As a legacy of the war, no coloured china was being made when I got married, so Queen Mary, deciding on a present to give me, reckoned a pretty tea service was the right thing. Imagine the excitement when a large box arrived from Marlborough House. Inside was a very poorly painted tea service with an old English pattern of violets. The box bore an old and tatty label: 'From His Royal Highness the Maharaja of Jaipur.' How I wish I had kept that box. The tea service is treasured but never used.

Barbara MacArthur with fellow recruits during the passing-out parade at the police training camp, Mill Reece, Staffordshire

Woman in BLUE

What was it like to be a policewoman sixty years ago? **BARBARA MacARTHUR,** *one of the first women to join Cardiff City Police, looks back*

In the early 1950s I decided to join the police force. After thirteen weeks' training at a camp in Mill Reece, Staffordshire, I returned to Cardiff. I was assigned to 'A' Division in the City Centre, which included some of the Tiger Bay (docks) area, and started to pound the beat.

We mainly patrolled singly, and with no mobile phones we were very much on our own. Women constables were not allowed to carry truncheons or handbags – when we patrolled dark areas our only consolation was the heavy black rubber torch which we usually carried up our jacket sleeve.

I believe I was one of the first policewomen in Cardiff and children used to refer to me as 'the lady policeman with the bun'. Prostitutes and pimps called me 'Lady Barbara'.

I was paid about £7 per week plus 3/6d boot allowance. The men got a little more. I was issued with two pairs of white cotton gloves to direct traffic. When it rained I used to amuse motorists by taking them off and wringing them out.

We weren't allowed to use make-up and we had to wear highly polished boots with thick navy-blue lisle stockings. The men wore waterproof police helmets, but the women had flat felt caps that absorbed the rain, as did the stockings, which was most uncomfortable. We were issued with 'sensible', over-sized, thick navy-blue knickers that reached from our chest to our knees. As we were not allowed to wear trousers this was just as well, in case we took a tumble during a scuffle.

Constables were not allowed to remove their thick serge belted jackets, even in the midst of summer. I did disobey that rule once when attending to a lady who'd suffered an epileptic fit and fallen down. I knelt down on the pavement, rolled up my jacket and placed it under her head. Still on my knees, I leant over to remove her false teeth, but realised that the surrounding crowd could read, in large print right across the back of my blue cotton shirt, the words 'PROPERTY OF CARDIFF CITY POLICE'.

One of my first duties was to escort prisoners to and from prison. Once I was told to collect two boys from the cells in the Cardiff Law Courts and take them to Llanrumney Hall Remand Home. When I went to collect the 'boys' I found they were well-built six-footers, who grinned when they saw their five-foot-six 'escort'. We delivered them safely at the Hall just in time for their tea.

I was co-opted to the vice squad, where one of my assignments was watching and raiding a brothel. The squad resented having a woman on the team and more than doubted my abilities. I was told to stand at the top of the stairs and on no account to let anyone pass me. When a twenty-stone bruiser charged me I thought, 'Blow this!' and at the very last minute stepped aside. He flew through the air and landed at the foot of the stairs with a loud thump. The squad rushed out of the bedrooms, patted me on the back and said, 'Good work!' I didn't tell them the truth...

We women were able to get information to pass on to the CID, as we would use the council toilets and chat with the ladies in charge who told us the latest news provided by local prostitutes and others. Also, when on duty in certain streets, we could get useful information from the prostitutes. I was once carpeted by our lady inspector for 'being too friendly and chatting to prostitutes before moving them on'. Also for being too polite on the job – tapping suspects on the shoulder and saying 'Excuse me' before arresting them. Another time I was told off for saying 'I'm sorry, I have to arrest you for...' I was told by the inspector that I should never be sorry about making an arrest.

M ost of my male colleagues were OK – but not all. For instance, one burly sergeant would often put his arm around me or pat me on the bottom. For a while I ignored it until one day, when he grabbed me, I started to tickle him. To my surprise he became absolutely helpless. He fell to the floor and I fell on top of him – but didn't stop tickling him. All the men were laughing until, suddenly, the inspector in charge walked in. I believe he must have known what was going on because he just ignored us and didn't say a word.

Another of our duties, called 'showing the uniform', was meant to be a deterrent. We were to patrol an area but not arrest or report anyone unless absolutely necessary. On one occasion I was told to patrol the castle grounds as reports had been made of 'peeping toms' watching 'courting couples'. I noticed a couple near some bushes with a man hiding behind a tree watching them. I shouted loudly

to warn the couple 'Someone is watching you!' To my surprise, two red-faced men ran out, adjusting their trousers. Another time I came across an American sailor who had had a few too many and was trying to sleep it off on a park bench. Unfortunately he had forgotten to button his flies. We had been instructed to arrest any drunken American sailors and hand them over to the American shore patrol temporarily based at the police station in the Law Courts. I didn't want to get him into trouble. The buttoning was complicated so I pinned up his flies with a couple of safety pins. Later, I wondered what he thought when he sobered up and saw the pins.

The American shore patrol regarded WPCs with some derision. One of them once said to me 'Ever been in a bar-room brawl, ma'am? Ha ha!' I think they thought we were there just for decoration. Once I had

Our lady inspector told me off for being too polite on the job – for tapping suspects on the shoulder and saying 'Excuse me' before arresting them

to arrest two men in town for two different offences. A police car arrived and we took them to the police station. There were shore patrol officers on each side of the entrance, twirling their night-sticks. My male colleague had a big grin on his face when he saw the open-mouthed Americans watch me drag both prisoners by their arms into the cop shop.

I n retrospect, I realise the reason I joined was not just because I wanted to do useful work, but also because I was quiet and shy and suffered from a lack of self-esteem. I wanted to jump into the deep-end of a job where I would be forced to gain some self-confidence. As a police officer I found I was not the person I thought I was, and soon discovered that I revelled in dealing with danger and with situations that demanded split-second decisions and prompt action. I was sorry to leave the force and thoroughly enjoyed my time there.

PEDANTS' REVOLT

Infuriating jargon, tired clichés and other bugbears which make Oldie readers reach for pen and paper...

ONE OFTEN comes across a sentence in a newspaper in which the grammar confuses the meaning, sometimes with comic effect. A leading article in the *Daily Telegraph* commenting on John Prescott's departure from the Privy Council was a particularly good example: 'The council numbers about 300 people, so Mr Prescott's maunderings are unlikely to be missed. After punching a voter during the 2001 election campaign, Tony Blair said: "John is John."'
MICHAEL SMITH

WHY, AND IN what circumstances, do people say, 'Wake up and smell the coffee'? There is no coffee in my household until at least 11am and, when there is any, I am the person who makes it. What can it mean? Am I out of touch?
ADRIAN WILLIAMS

INSPECTOR LEWIS missed a vital clue recently. A character purporting to be an Oxford Professor of English said, 'I feel like I've had my life on pause' and 'if you feel like I do'. Obviously an impostor.
STEPHEN ALDHOUSE

WHY, WHEN I take my item to the till, does the person taking my money say, 'That will be £10 [or whatever the sum is] altogether'? Altogether? For one item?
MARY BURGERHOUT

THE RECENT habit of adding 'way' to so many words is driving me mad. Do I come down the roadway, park on my driveway, walk up the pathway and enter the hallway? No! I come down the road, park on my drive, walk up the path and enter the hall.
Is this obsession part of a transatlantic creep, or just a British banality?
HATTIE BRANTWOOD

I BOMBED THE *Scharnhorst*

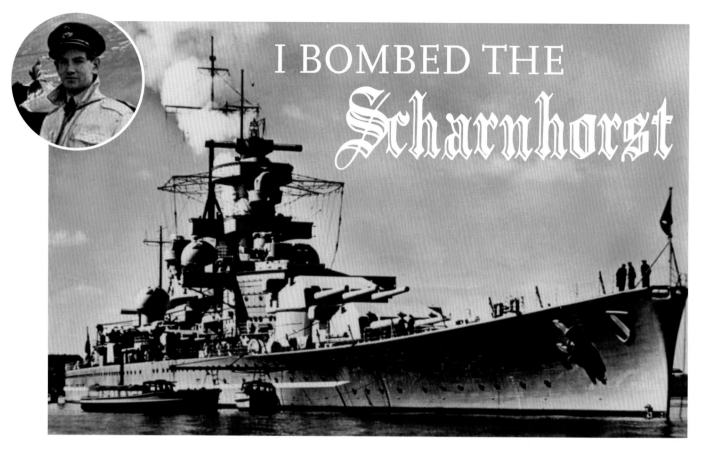

Above: The battle-cruiser *Scharnhorst*. Inset: Pilot Officer Hugh O'Neill

Loading up with coffee, biscuits and a basket of pigeons, **HUGH O'NEILL** *and his crew took off to attack the German Navy's prize battleship...*

The discovery by a team of Norwegian underwater explorers of the German-built battle-cruiser *Scharnhorst* lying many fathoms below the surface of the North Sea was the subject of a recent television documentary. The ship had been sunk by Admiral Sir Bruce Fraser and the British Home Fleet in December 1943. This put an end to a period of serious menace, which included the sinking of the aircraft carrier *Glorious* and a successful dash up the English Channel from St Nazaire, during which Lieutenant-Commander Eugene Esmonde won a posthumous VC for his Swordfish attack. The sight of the remains of this elegant ship lying on the sea bed stirred some earlier memories. Mine were of a cloudless day off the Norwegian coast on 21st June 1940, when four of us flew in close formation to bomb the ship from 10,000 feet in the face of heavy

anti-aircraft fire and an air escort of German fighters.

The day started at Leuchars in Scotland, where preparations were being made for our four aircraft – American-built Lockheed Hudsons – to fly up to Sumburgh in Shetland. We would stay there for a few days, and the

> **It seemed discourteous not to reply to their signal, so I flashed 'Guten Morgen' on our Aldis lamp**

senior officer's aircraft carried a case of whisky to keep out the damp and cold. All was being arranged in an orderly manner, when the telephone rang in the Operations Room with a message that the *Scharnhorst* had left its Norwegian base in Trondheim Fjord and was sailing south down the coast with surface and air escort. We were ordered to find and

bomb it 'on the way' to Shetland.

Each of the Hudsons was hastily armed with two 500 lb semi-armour-piercing bombs, and a Lewis gun was laid on a bed which had been installed in the cabin of each aircraft. A modification allowing it to be mounted and fired out of the open cabin windows had been put in hand some weeks before, augmenting the two Browning machine-guns in the rear turret.

Coffee, biscuits and a basket of pigeons were loaded on board, the latter being deployed for message duty in the event of a descent into the sea. The method of attack was agreed with our leader, Squadron Leader D Y Feeny, and we set off to join our aircraft. Pilot Officer 'Ralph' Lynn and I had tossed up beforehand to decide who would fly the aircraft – a traditional practice to avoid a rush to be at the wheel – and I lost. My responsibility as co-pilot would be to navigate, drop the bombs, fire the Lewis gun and dispense the coffee and biscuits. Lynn and I were joined by Sergeants Steel and Cliff, the wireless operator and air-gunner, and we all climbed aboard. Our average age was 19, but we were old hands by now, having been in the squadron since before the war. We regarded the *Scharnhorst* affair as a bit of a lark, and were looking forward to a sight of the great ship.

Our four aircraft set off in wide formation from Leuchars in a gentle climb towards Norway, and things on board were fairly relaxed. I busied myself with the navigation charts, and the rear-gunner tested his guns. The pigeons were settled in their basket and the shiny Lewis gun was loaded and ready for action.

We arrived at the island of Utsaire, just off the Norwegian coast, and closed up into tight formation, turning northwards to begin our search for the German ships. We were in position 'in the box' behind and below the leader. There was a good sea running, with plenty of foam, so we had to concentrate pretty closely at 10,000 feet to pick out the enemy ships. A hot sun shone into the cockpit from a cloudless sky, and we communicated with each other in the formation by 'zogging', transmitting Morse code out of the window by use of the forearm.

The flash of a signal lamp and a burst of anti-aircraft fire ahead and at our level brought us up sharply. And there they were – sleek, grey shapes plunging through the rough sea on their way down to the Fatherland and families in Kiel. It seemed discourteous not to reply to their signal, so I flashed 'Guten Morgen' on our Aldis lamp on the off-chance that an unpleasant reception might be delayed. Meanwhile, Feeny had opened his bomb doors and we followed suit, carrying out our plan to 'pattern-bomb' the ships.

The ships took immediate avoiding action, altering course independently and bringing their anti-aircraft armament into full play. Feeny's aircraft was hit almost at once and began to trail black smoke. By now the *Scharnhorst* was turning sharply almost below us: she appeared to be on fire from stem to stern, such was the effect of all her guns in action. At the same time, a series of black dots low over the ships – which we

had naively taken for balloons – revealed themselves as a fighter escort, ascending rapidly towards us to deal with the threat to their favourite battle-cruiser.

By now, the formation was breaking up in the hail of anti-aircraft fire, and as Feeny had failed to drop any bombs, there seemed little point in carrying on with our plan to 'pattern-bomb'. I sprang into the nose and released our salvo in the hope that it might go down somebody's funnel. I sensed an opportunity to use the Lewis gun, so with a grin at Lynn, who was steady at the controls, I returned to the cabin and mounted the gun on its peg in a window. Before leaving the cockpit I saw that Feeny's aircraft was blazing well, while the others were obscured in the pall of gunfire smoke which hung in the sky. One of these was later confirmed as shot down.

The first of the Me 109s came lazily past alongside, its green-and-white colour scheme set against the white of the pilot's helmet. I waved the Lewis gun at him with a flourish, and staggered back into the cabin from its recoil. The fighter carried on undeterred and delivered a *coup de grâce* to Feeny's aircraft, which rolled over and disappeared in a welter of smoke and flame. There was an enormous explosion and our Hudson filled with acrid smoke. When it cleared, I saw through the cabin window that a large piece of our wiring and aileron had been shot away by a direct hit, and fuel was streaming from a holed fuel tank.

Making sure that the pigeons were not too startled by this turn of events, I went forwards to appraise Lynn of the situation, and we both raised our eyebrows as he struggled to keep the aircraft on an even keel.

'They seem to outgrow their iPods and iPhones so quickly these days...'

Fate then took a hand. One moment we were sitting ducks in the clear sky as the fighters lined up to have another go at us, and then we were suddenly enveloped in a thin layer of altostratus cloud which had formed off the coast. This piece of luck enabled us to set course away from the scene of action and size up the damage to the aircraft. Emerging from the clouds after twenty minutes or so, we found ourselves alone in the sky, nursing our damaged Hudson and discussing over welcome coffee and biscuits how best to get down on the ground in one piece, provided we had enough fuel left to make a landfall.

In *The Drama of the Scharnhorst*, Fritz-Otto Busch revealed that the expenditure of ammunition during this action from the *Scharnhorst* alone was 900 rounds of 4.1 in, 1,200 rounds of 37 mm and 2,400 rounds of 20 mm shells. He goes on to describe how the ship was ordered by Group West to put into Stavanger after the action, much to the annoyance of its captain. We, on the other hand, had put into Sumburgh, coming to rest in an untidy heap on the airfield. Not only had we sustained a fair amount of damage from the ships, but the Me 109 had put a few rounds into our cabin and through the propeller blades. It had been a duffer's shot, and we had been lucky.

Much to our dismay, the detachment whisky had gone down with Feeny, but the resident Coastal Command Blenheim flight at Sumburgh counselled us with a dram or two. Shortly afterwards a Fleet Air Arm Walrus amphibian appeared out of the blue. Flown by Lieutenant Derek Matthew RN, it had been catapulted from a cruiser in the middle of a North Sea battle and could not be recovered. He decided that Sumburgh was the best place for him and, after hearing our tale of derring-do, declared the cockpit of his Walrus to be his wardroom, and we piled in for further counselling from naval supplies.

We raised our glasses to Dunstan Feeny and his crew and then to Captain Hoffman of the *Scharnhorst*, wishing him bon voyage until the next time. Soon it would be the turn of Admiral Sir Bruce Fraser.

Having made sure that the pigeons would be properly watered and fed, I went off to fish a hill loch.

'Brussels wants companies to be more inclusive, so our board has been enlarged with one heroin addict and one member of the Flat Earth Society'

'Don't take failure lying down, Hoskins – always blame someone else!'

'I see from your CV that your top score on "Alien Zombie Attack" is 56,849'

'When the music stops, sit down in the nearest chair. Whoever doesn't get a chair will be made redundant'

The **Oldie** AT THE OFFICE

'Jeez, if you're going to cry about it, keep your stupid job'

'Hmmm... impressive CV...'

BORE TV (See Digital Channel 356)
This week's highlights 24th–31st December 2013

❖ THE RUBBISH PROGRAMME
Channel 5, Christmas Day, 8pm
The team visits the Doncaster home of retired social worker Yasser Lipman whose two-storey house is filled with wheelie bins crammed with hundreds of copies of *Radio Times*. (R,S,HD)

❖ WHO DID YOU SAY YOU ARE?
Channel 4, December 29th, 7:30pm
Fiona has a B&B in the Orkneys. She suffers acute memory difficulties which seriously affect the day-to-day running of the house. These include guests arriving to find they have no room or that they are double booked. Kishwar Bahi investigates. (R,S,HD)

❖ MEERKAT HOSPITAL
BBC One, December 27th, 9pm
Idi is still having trouble with his injured left leg and Dr Samgrass thinks he may have to amputate. And Arifa's babies are two weeks overdue and she is being tube-fed. Presenter Dashni Warrender. (R,S,HD)

NEW SERIES

❖ AND SO TO BID
BBC Four, Boxing Day, 6:05pm
Antique furniture experts Bob Walling and Andy Bent scour the auction rooms of Devon to find the perfect four-poster bed and try to outbid each other in getting the best bargain. (R,S,HD)

❖ POSTMAN PATRICIA
BBC Three, New Year's Eve, 11:30am
In 2012 Dublin postman Patrick Gorman had a sex change operation. Back at work, Patricia encounters a number of problems resuming relationships with colleagues, not all of whom are sympathetic. (R,S,HD)

PICK OF THE WEEK

❖ CELEBRITY CHRISTMAS CARDS
BBC Two, Christmas Eve, 9pm
Caroline Flack is invited by a number of celebrities to see who has sent them Christmas cards. Her hosts include Charles Saatchi, Stephen Fry, Bradley Wiggins and Anna Ford. (R,S,HD)

❖ WHO WANTS TO BE IN SNOW BUSINESS?
ITV2, Christmas Day, 8pm
Edgy stand-up Jimmy Carr fronts this seasonal game show where families compete to build the biggest snowman against the clock. The prize is a week in Oslo. (R,S,HD)

❖ WE MUST BE NOMAD
ITV4, December 28th, 5pm
Julian and Diana spent a year travelling in the Gobi Desert with a tribe of nomads. They are now attempting to re-live their experience in a home-made yurt in the Isle of Man. This week, their camel, Urtak, gives birth to a baby boy. (Episode 3 of 9.) (R,S,HD)

An AFGHAN journey

*As director of the charity Afghan Connection, **SARAH FANE** is a regular visitor to Afghanistan, this most beautiful, vast and complex of countries*

*Photographs by **SARAH FANE***

For over half my life I have been visiting Afghanistan. As a medical student I worked in a maternity unit in the tribal badlands of the North-West Frontier Province. Returning as a doctor during the Soviet war, I lived with the Mujahideen, visiting patients by horseback in the refugee camps along the Afghan border. Under the Taliban, I travelled across a country desecrated by 23 years of war to work in a mother–child clinic, and since 2001 I have visited twice yearly as director for the charity Afghan Connection, which I set up to support education, health and cricket in Afghanistan. Its vast, diverse landscapes, hospitable people and infuriatingly complex nature have etched their way into my soul. AC has built 36 schools in Afghanistan and now supports education for a

population of 80,000 in the district of Worsaj in the Hindu Kush. A direct benefit of my many visits is the tremendous bond of trust I have managed to forge with Afghan people. This allows me to stay in remote villages where, each evening, the headman comes to greet me, takes my hand in his and reassures me that it is his honour to protect my security.

There are now regular flights from Dubai to Kabul, packed with tough-looking, muscled, tattooed security guys. Once famous for its gardens, Kabul has become a fortress city, constantly on alert for terrorist activity, riddled with check points, dwarfed by watch towers, a city of vulnerability and suspicion, ringed by barbed wire and concrete road blocks. The magnificent road north over the beautiful Salang Pass, through the highest mountain tunnel in the world, is no longer considered safe for us to travel on,

so when I last visited we flew up over the Hindu Kush in a tiny single-engined plane, almost scraping the great leathery spines of the mountains as we went. A dramatic landing on Taloqan's dusty runway and our journey to Worsaj began.

This took us along a dusty track which runs beside the Korcha River through snow-capped mountains and dramatic gorges, past scenes unchanged over the centuries. Oxen pull ancient wooden ploughs; women and children, bent double in their brightly coloured clothes, harvest potatoes in the fields; turbaned men in striped green and purple coats edged in red embroidery toss beans into the air with huge pitch-forks, stirring up great clouds of dust, and pack their produce into sacks, loading them onto the colourful woven saddles of their donkeys.

PHOTOGRAPHS © SARAH FANE

When we arrived at the first school we ever built, hundreds of girls were patiently waiting for us. Nothing could have prepared us for the exuberant reception we received: garlands tossed over our heads, confetti flung from a hundred tiny hands, singing, clapping and bouquets of plastic flowers thrust into our arms. The hospitality is overwhelming: everywhere we go, we are invited to eat – whether it be freshly picked apples, pears and peaches on carpets laid out under the poplars by the mountain streams, or feasts shared with teachers or homeowners, where goat meat, mutton, chicken, guinea fowl, sparrow, trout, rice, flat breads, salads and stews are served on vast mats laid out on pristine carpets. The men sit and eat with us, their women kept firmly behind walls to avoid meeting male visitors. I am lucky to be accepted by the men, and then head to the women's quarters, where I share their laughter and gossip. The challenge is to eat all that is presented and to eat just the right amount, for if you fail to eat enough, they think you do not like it, and if you finish, you are given more, knowing that just a few hours later another generous host will lavish more food upon you. We sleep on toshaks on the floor, have little chance to wash and have not one second of privacy, but all the time we are aware of the immense privilege it is to witness community life in Afghanistan and to stay at the heart of these families.

Fridays are holidays when schools are closed and outings planned. This time it was a trip to some beautiful lakes, once a popular tourist destination. Pots and oil and rice and tea are loaded onto the vehicles. The journey leads us up the valley towards the distant Anjoman Pass and the Panjshir Valley beyond. Teachers join the trip at the last village, armed with fishing nets to catch our lunch. At last we round the corner and see the famous lakes ahead. We race down the hillside through the bright red flowers, towards the glacial waters. The backdrop is magnificent, with villages clinging precariously to the mountainside just beneath the snow line and the lake stretching for miles before

dropping over the edge of a massive crevasse into a cascading waterfall.

We drive on until we reach a flood plain, where we lay rugs and cushions out on the grass. We are surrounded by mountains and rivers and streams. Some of the men search for firewood and set up camp, while others fish or make tea, and the lazier ones swim and play volleyball in the sunshine. The fish soon arrive – a mixture of big rainbow trout caught in the lake and much

smaller river trout. They are gutted, laid out on the bonnet of the car and salted in the sunshine. Soon we have a delicious picnic of fresh fish and rice.

It was an inspiring trip, and most wonderful of all is the thought that in Worsaj, where barely a woman of my age can read or write, every child is now going to school. For as long as this is happening, there must be hope for the future of Afghanistan, and hope too that tourists will return one day.

SOLD, *to the lowest bidder*

Down the pub in **WINIFRED FOLEY**'s *mining village,*
old Jarge's chicken was up for auction...

Illustration by Peter Bailey

We didn't have a proper idiot in our tiny mining village 80 years ago, but we had a good sprinkling of simpletons. Old Jarge was one of them. He had been conned by two wily brothers into marrying their deaf and dumb sister Liza, in return for the free tenancy of a hovel of a cottage they could have rented out for two shillings a week.

Somewhere in his grizzled old head Jarge had a brain, but it worked in a very low gear. As one of his pit mates observed, 'If you ask old Jarge what day it is on a Monday, by the time he worked it out 'twould be Tuesday.'

With a grand swagger, Jarge put the fattened bird on the table. He was almost beside himself

His slowness of speech barred him from conversation and made him ob-sessively envious of his ready-tongued mates. He had, however, collected an extensive vocabulary of obscenities, crude jokes and insults, for the miners were sort of bilingual, using one language in front of women and children, and another of uninhibited vulgarity down the pit. On the whole Jarge was a placid-tempered old chap, but he suffered a lot from Liza's inade-quacies – atrocious cooking, poor domestic skills, allowing her pet hens to come indoors to eat the crumbs from on top of the table as well as underneath it.

When Jarge annoyed her she would get hold of one of his ears in her bony, claw-like hand and shake his head till his eyes rolled. Jarge would then swear at her with every obscenity and insult he had gathered, knowing they fell on deaf ears but giving his anger some release.

All was forgiven when Liza gave him his nightly twopence for his half-pint of cider. It would last him all evening in the male refuge, a humble little pub at the bottom of the village. Although he could not join in, Jarge loved to listen to the banter and arguments of his mates. One evening he

was overwhelmed by the drama and cleverness of two men arguing over the price of a ewe. The seller was asking 35 shillings, but only one customer was affluent enough to bargain with him. Soon all the men in the pub became involved, with plenty of comment on the characters of the two protagonists.

After almost an hour Jarge was beside himself with excitement as the bargaining reached a climax. The seller said his lowest figure was now 27 shillings and sixpence. The would-be buyer hesitated, then appeared to lose interest. 'Tell you what then, you mingy bugger,' fumed the ewe owner, 'I'll split the difference. Give me 25 shillings and the ewe is yours.'

The deal was done and the excitement over, but not for Jarge. 'Split the difference, split the difference' – he could not get the glory of the incident out of his mind. If only he had something to sell!

It took a long time for an idea to germinate in Jarge's skull. He stole one of Liza's hens and put her in a single coop, hidden by a piece of rusty corrugated iron. Jarge got thinner as the hen got fatter on Liza's culinary efforts, sneaked out in his jacket, and he dug plenty of worms from his garden. Near to Christmas, he went out under cover of darkness and wrung the hen's neck. With twopence jangling in his pocket, he went down to the pub and, with a grand swagger, put the fattened bird on the table.

There was immediate interest, and Jarge was almost beside himself as the bidding started. 'Dooan't take any notice o' the bugger,' was the unanimous advice for the first offer of threepence. Gradually, by twopences and three-pences, rivalry drove the bird's price up to the grand total of half-a-crown. No more was forthcoming; Jarge's moment of glory had come. His blue eyes wet with emotion, and the veins standing out on his forehead, he brought his fist down hard enough to spill the cider from some newly filled glasses.

'Split the difference,' he bellowed. 'Give I one and sixpence.'

'With the economy as it is, I'm putting all my money into pigs'

770965 25001

HOME FRONT
ALICE PITMAN

OUR SUBURBAN semi has been transformed into an infirmary. For weeks we have been plagued with afflictions, both real and imagined. Before Christmas I was struck down with a prolapsed disc in my lower back. It was triggered by a sneeze: one moment I was contentedly reading *The Noël Coward Diaries* in bed – oddly enough, his account of a slipped disc he had in the 1950s – the next, I was seized by an explosion of agony to rival childbirth. I screamed so much that the dog ran out of the room and son Fred poked his head round the door to tell me to be quiet: 'It's actually really annoying,' he said. I became quite deranged and accused him of being a psychopath with no empathy. Minutes later, he sheepishly returned and asked in a small voice whether there was anything he could do to help. So I sent him to the Co-op to get some painkillers (which were nowhere near as effective as the eight injections of Novocaine the Master had).

I had six appointments with a chiropractor over the following fortnight. Each session cost £42 and lasted no more than quarter of an hour. When the money ran dry, but the pain didn't, I hobbled off to the doctor who referred me to a physiotherapist at Leatherhead Hospital: 'I wouldn't waste any more money on a chiropractor. You'd be better off getting your husband to massage your back.' Which, to my complete surprise, he did. The children were appalled at the sight of Mr HF rubbing almond oil along my spine (as was I when he suddenly leaned over and whispered 'How's about that then?' in the voice of Jimmy Savile).

No sooner had I recovered than Mr HF was laid up for two weeks with what he insisted on calling tendonitis, but which I suspect was gout (he loses his temper if I suggest as much). He insisted that the only way he could recover was to keep his leg horizontal – i.e. lie in bed all day, issuing food and drink orders like Albert Steptoe.

At least both these ailments were real. Son Fred, on the other hand, now

'Could you check my printer's plugged in while you're down there?'

believes his days are numbered. When not stacking shelves at Waitrose, he seems to spend most of his gap year surfing the internet looking for things to find wrong with himself. Consequently he has conjured up a whole host of imagined illnesses and deadly diseases. First he thought he had skin cancer as he was sure a mole on his arm had gone a funny colour. Then he thought he might be HIV positive after cutting his foot in the sea at Brighton (he got it into his head he must have stepped on a discarded needle). Then there was his tapeworm, followed by Type 2 diabetes.

The latest is – of all things – asbestosis, after finding out our now demolished garage possessed an asbestos roof. 'But I used to climb up there to get my cricket ball!' Telling him I was practically raised on asbestos did little to reassure him (the Aged P stockpiled those asbestos heat-insulating plates when she got wind of the impending ban). Then a grim website where 'asbestovision goggles' allowed Fred to see the 'hidden dangers' in a typical pre-1990s property convinced him our entire house – built just after the war – was a veritable asbestos show-home.

He has become so annoying about it, I have banned him from ever mentioning the A word again. The Aged P is amused by the whole thing. 'His grandfather was an appalling hypochondriac too.' Fred's friends also see the funny side. After an evening in the pub during which he had revealed his anxieties, his pal James texted him a picture of a man on his death bed with Fred's face superimposed, above a slogan which read: 'Not long now, Fred.'

What isn't long now is his trip to China. He is bored out of his mind at Asbestos Towers and certainly more than ready for it. Whether the Chinese are ready for Fred is another thing entirely.

Explosive stuff

Peddling dynamite in West Africa can be a tricky business, says **ANTHONY WEALE**

Illustration by Nick Baker

Most people go into the explosives business with a background in mining, science or the army. I became a dynamite salesman through bottle manufacture and cardboard boxes, then neckties and ladies' underwear, and finally worsted suitings. There was some logic to my aimless wandering through the department store of life: a wise industrialist once told me never to stay in any position for longer than two years, to avoid being found out; he also advised me to work for a multinational, as there would generally be an escape route.

My escape was to West Africa, selling explosives – not military explosives, but the kind of stuff that is used in mines and quarries. Twenty-five years ago, most commercial explosives were based on nitroglycerine, which is sensitive to shock, heat and sometimes

even to vibration. It is, to put it mildly, capricious. In the tropics, NG-based explosives deteriorate quite quickly; your stick of dynamite starts to leak, first chemical salts, then pure NG – when it becomes dangerous.

I was posted to Liberia because nobody else wanted the job. I arrived in the White Man's Graveyard during the wet season, those few months when rain falls for weeks on end and thunder rumbles interminably. In the darkness the sky constantly flickers with sheet lightning.

Some weeks later I left my wife and offspring in a bungalow beside the fetid Farmington River and set off alone for Cameroon. Late the following evening, I landed in Douala, a port in the Bight of Biafra. It was hot and humid, and there was a strong smell of sewage and burning charcoal. After the officious tedium of immigration and customs, I managed to find

a clapped-out yellow taxi – all taxis in West Africa are yellow and all are clapped-out – and negotiated a fare to the only hotel I had heard of, the Beau Séjour, a well-known knocking shop, as I later discovered when a thinly clad girl groped me on the stairs. Optimistically, I had telexed for a room.

The cab lurched and jolted towards the town centre with little input from the driver, who lounged in the front seat and chatted with passing acquaintances. At the hotel I was pestered by small boys, whose idea of an evening on the town was to deprive me of my luggage. The man at the desk had never heard of me or my booking, and threw my telex on the floor with disdain. I sat on a damp and smelly sofa for the rest of the night. The lights were dim, the small boys had vanished and I waited gloomily for dawn. A hot, portly man, who never said a word but continually scratched himself, used me as a pillow.

This was a typical arrival in West Africa, and one that was repeated with depressing regularity. I never learned to manage it better. The dynamite pedlar is a solitary and often melancholy creature, who rarely admits what he does for a living. He travels light and for obvious reasons carries no samples. The authorities in each country don't like his wares, don't trust his intentions and don't believe a word he says. Mostly they are in the pockets of French manufacturers and agents. Trying to sell explosives in French West Africa, as my father pithily put it, is like digging for oysters in the Sahara. One thing is certain: you can accomplish nothing without a good agent. I was in Cameroon, where my company had not made a single sale since before the last war, to find such an agent.

I found my way to the British Consulate to discuss my problem with a junior diplomat, who had impeccable manners and a hangover, and was clearly out of his depth in the world of mines and quarries. He directed me to the British Chamber of Commerce, who were equally helpless and aimed me towards a bank. All day I was shuffled from one office to another, from insurance companies to agricultural implement stockists. But one name kept cropping up: I must track down Nfon Mukete, Chairman of the Cameroon Development Corporation.

I set off through the dirty streets to find his office. On the way, a stark naked madman with mud in his hair attempted to hijack my briefcase. We strained and tugged at it all the way to the office door, when he gave up the attempt and ran off, cackling and waving his arms about. Might I see the Nfon? No, I might not; he was in Victoria, about forty miles away.

The following morning, after a good night's sleep – I had bribed the man at the hotel, who had found me a room, and we were now the best of friends – I did an early deal with a taxi driver, booking him for the whole day to go wherever might be necessary in pursuit of the Nfon (a Nfon is a Cameroonian chief). First to Victoria, with its black sands, at the foot of Mount Cameroon. But Nfon Mukete had moved on to

The dynamite pedlar is a solitary creature. He travels light and for obvious reasons carries no samples. The authorities in each country don't like his wares

Buea, twenty miles away. Off we clattered, me stabbed repeatedly by a loose spring poking through the upholstery. The Nfon had moved on again, to Bamenda. We reached Bamenda in due course, ploughing through the town, scattering muddy hens which seemed to have been prematurely plucked, mangy dogs and skinny children, and swung into a yard smothered by bougainvillea. The driver waved me towards a large, shabby house with a verandah, and composed himself to sleep.

There was nobody about, so I quietly crossed the verandah and went into the hallway. A door was open on my right, and at a large mahogany table littered with papers sat an elderly man in a Kinte cloth, one of those elegant togas worn by West African gentlemen. He looked up over his spectacles and said, 'Good afternoon, my dear fellow. You'll stay for lunch, I hope. You're Mr Weale, I believe, and I'm Dr Mukete.'

He cleared away his papers, a big girl laid the table and I ate my first good meal in Cameroon – roast lamb

with potatoes and spiced greens, with a bottle of cold claret, which the Nfon and I shared. His wife and various relations stood by, watching as we ate and urging us on to greater efforts.

When the plates had been cleared away, we had what I believed was a constructive chat. The Nfon seemed keen, and just the man for me – he spoke perfect English and had a doctorate in botany from Manchester University. He would, on receipt of a formal agency agreement signed by me, set about building an explosives magazine to comply with the laws of the land, and I would ship a few tons of 'powder', as we dynamite pedlars always call it. The Nfon and I would make our fortunes. We shook hands warmly on our arrangement.

A few days later, after I had travelled to the capital to inform the Cameroonian Department of Mines and the British Embassy what I was up to, I returned to Liberia and my abandoned family and after consultation with my lawyer in Monrovia wrote my formal letter, very pleased with myself and full of hope, planning to return to Cameroon shortly to tie up any loose ends.

I never saw Nfon Mukete again. When I got back to Cameroon a few weeks later, I heard that he had been clapped in jail for what was rumoured to be high treason. This seemed unlikely. Perhaps he had got wind of a plot and went for a sabbatical. I never got to the bottom of it. Nearly seven years later, in an office in Mexico City (I had escaped again), I received a letter from Nfon Mukete dated three months earlier. It had been sent to my old address in Liberia, then forwarded to my company, then to the Foreign Office, to which I had been attached as a debt collector, and so in the diplomatic bag to Mexico. It began:

'Dear Weale, I have been thinking about our most stimulating discussion after lunch the other day, and have come to the conclusion that there is every prospect of a mutually profitable association. I would be most grateful if you would send me further technical information as to exactly how to build an explosives magazine...'

FRIENDSHIP
through the fence

'Harry' loved to hear good news but took sorrow in her stride, reasoning that 'the Lord fits the back to the burden'. **URSULA HOLDEN** *remembers her next-door neighbour*

Mrs Harrison was our neighbour when we moved to Chiswick in the Fifties. From the start she made it clear that she and her elderly husband needed quiet – meaning that our two small daughters should not make a noise when they played in our backyard. They liked splashing water about.

Soon Mrs Harrison became 'Harry'. We talked daily through a gap in the fence.

Unless it rained we used washing lines for drying clothes; washing machines were expensive and not for the likes of us. We burned coal fires, chopping wood for kindling or buying it in bundles from Tucker, the coal man, who called with his lorry each week. In wet weather, to gain attention, Harry would lean through the gap to beat on our back door with a stick.

The Harrisons rented the ground floor. Harry slept in the front room on a divan. Jack, her husband, shared the back room with their son, Peter. They had a small kitchen and an outside loo.

We had the whole house, taking in lodgers and supplying them with partial board. When our third child was born, I tried not to shriek too loudly, but Harry said she heard and felt everything through the thin wall.

Cooking was her preferred topic. 'What you having for your dinner then?' was her favourite question. Her own cooking was her pride, her scones were second to none. Roasts, jam roly-poly and sponges were beyond me. Stews, fries or sandwiches were so easy. Over the years I learned to cook, ignoring the children's accusations: 'You've been putting something into this.' Of course I had.

Experimenting was more fun than a conventional recipe. Fortunately they liked school dinners.

Peter Harrison was older than our children. He did well in business studies, working for a time in Ghana. Harry and I were mystified by some spices he brought back. Garam masala stayed untouched in my cupboard for years.

Harry calmed my fears when, one by one, our daughters left home for further education. 'That girl will be all right. I can tell.'

Cooking was her preferred topic. 'What you having for your dinner then?' was her favourite question

I joined a class in creative writing, showing Harry my homework each week. 'Pretty good' was her usual verdict. Jack was more critical. I had put 'rotten bugger, rotten sod' in some dialogue. He said it was 'a bit too modern'. Clean language mattered.

Few in our road had telephones then. When Jack got ill and was an in-patient, the hospital got in touch with me on the morning of his death. I knocked on Harry's door: 'The hospital rang. I'm afraid it's bad news.' She sagged against the doorpost, weeping. There was much to arrange; the procedures following death took time. I stayed with her that day. She chose his coffin with care from the mid-price range; his funeral was small and dignified.

Harry adjusted to single life, sleeping in the front room as usual, leaving the back room ready for Peter, now married. His wife sent glowing accounts of the sumptuous meals she and Peter attended. All was reported through the fence. When their lovely son was born, his photograph was displayed near Harry's divan.

The child was small when Peter got stomach cancer. Harry said that she knew when she woke that morning: 'My Peter will die today.' And he did.

More sorrow followed. The little grandson died, aged eight. He fell, hitting his head on some seaside rocks.

She was realistic. Her own mother had warned her years back that married life would not all be a bed of roses. But 'the Lord fits the back to the burden'.

She loved to hear good news. 'There's you writing a book and Ann Tucker learning to drive a car.'

She sensed her approaching death when her turn came to be ill. 'You will follow me, won't you?' She meant would I join her cortège in the walk from the chapel to her waiting grave.

The bus was late. I arrived only in time to see her coffin being lowered down.

I like to remember her laughter when the rain spoilt our washing on the lines. 'Good thing cows don't fly.'

ILLUSTRATION BY PETER BAILEY

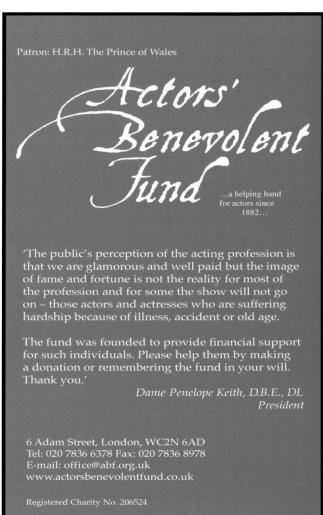

...ted swimming pool and bar

Emerald 'Sky', Passau

The Terrace

EUROPE'S NEWEST DELUXE
RIVER CRUISE COMPANY

...merald Waterways offers a new kind of river cruising experience. With a ...and new fleet complete with an array of spectacular ship innovations; ...credible itineraries filled with excursions; and so much included in the price ... our holidays, we offer the unique combination of amazing river cruises and ...ceptional value for money.

...VOLUTIONISING RIVER CRUISING

FABULOUS ONBOARD DINING & DRINKS

YOUR RELAXING RIVER RETREAT

...ike any other on Europe's ...ers, our brand new ships boast ...eated swimming pool which ...nsforms into a cinema in the ...enings. And to replace the run-of-...e-mill French Balcony found on ...her ships, we have the Emerald ...norama Balcony, complete with ...ecked area and open-air system. ...the touch of a button, the upper ...f of the cabin's floor-to-ceiling ...ndow drops down to let in fresh ...and provide full panoramic views ...the landscape.

As well as all delicious meals served in our ship's main restaurant, Reflections, when the weather's fine you can enjoy a light breakfast and café-style lunch alfresco on The Terrace - all included in the price of your holiday. Plus, you'll enjoy complimentary beer, wine and soft drinks with lunch and dinner at each of our venues - as well as tea and coffee available at all times throughout your cruise and bottled water restocked in your cabin daily, free of charge.

We offer a great choice of cabins, starting with the Emerald Stateroom - one of the biggest of its kind and great value for money. For those seeking a higher level of luxury, our Owner's One-bedroom Suites boast a separate bedroom and lounge; complimentary mini-bar re-stocked daily with wine, beer and soft drinks; Nespresso machine; and use of an iPad. Plus, you can order an included continental breakfast, pre-dinner canapés and after-dinner sweet treats to your suite too.

INCLUDED ON YOUR CRUISE

- Return scheduled flights from a choice of 5 UK airports
- All meals at Reflections
- Alfresco dining on The Terrace
- Onboard pool and cinema
- Complimentary wine, beer and soft drinks at lunch and dinner
- Unlimited tea and coffee
- Bottled water restocked daily
- Shore excursions almost every day
- Extra special experiences with Emerald**PLUS**
- Complimentary WiFi onboard
- All port charges & airport taxes
- All tips, saving you up to £440 per couple

2015 RIVER CRUISES	NOW from	SAVE pp
Nuremberg - Budapest 8 day river cruise	**£995**	£500
NEW Amsterdam - Basel 8 day river cruise	**£1,195**	£500
NEW Netherlands - Belgium 8 day river cruise	**£1,395**	£500
NEW Budapest - Bucharest 10 day river cruise & tour	**£1,695**	£500
Amsterdam - Budapest 15 day river cruise	**£1,995**	£500

Right now we're offering £500 per person off any 2015 river cruise - but hurry, availability is limited!

EMERALD
WATERWAYS

For your brochure, call free **0808 102 0329**
or visit **www.emeraldwaterways.co.uk**

EMERALD
W A T E R W A Y S

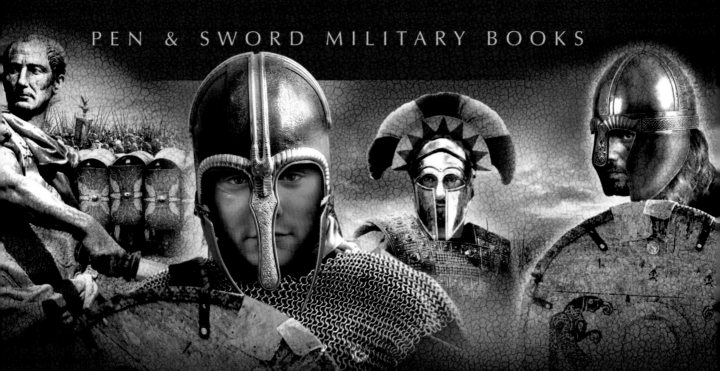

'They cannot be serious'